Tremble, fearful mortals, for the
midnight hour chimes.

Ancient battlefields echo to the clatter of bleached bones and rusted armour as the dead rise once more. Plague pits and shallow graves heave as maggot-eaten fingers tear aside the loose topsoil. The baying of lifeless wolves chills mortal souls to the core. Chiropteran horrors spill from tumbledown belfries as a shrieking cloud, bloated from a diet of fresh gore.

Yet all these fiends pale in comparison to the masters of the revenant host: the Soulblight vampires. These deathless warlords bear both the mightiest of powers and the most dreadful of curses. By their will can the necromantic arts be harnessed to bring hordes of undead warriors lurching to their feet. With a single blow can they tear through armour, flesh and bone to rip out the vital organs beneath. But to maintain their monstrous existence, a vampire must slake an endless thirst for the blood of the living. The beast within is demanding indeed, and behind the porcelain facade of humanity, vampires are ravenous horrors who would plunge the realms into an endless, abominable night.

The Soulblight vampires consider themselves destined to rule. In this, they reflect he whose malignant power sired them: Nagash, Supreme Lord of the Undead. From bleak Nagashizzar, he commands his Gravelords to march forth, bringing the curse of undeath to every corner of the realms. In the darkness of his necrotopia shall the vampires feast as never before, mortals reduced to cowering slaves fit only to be drained of blood. So it is that the Soulblight aristocracy makes war on the living with a relentless fervour, their corpse-hosts reinforced with the bodies of those same bold warriors who once defied them.

So be afraid, mortals, and clutch thy blessed trinkets close, for night draws in – and the Soulblight Gravelords come for thee.

CONTENTS

PRODUCED BY THE WARHAMMER STUDIO

With thanks to The Faithful for their additional playtesting services.

British Cataloguing-in-Publication Data. A catalogue record for this book is available from the British Library. Pictures used for illustrative purposes only.

Games Workshop Ltd., Willow Road, Lenton, Nottingham, NG7 2WS, United Kingdom

warhammer.com

The monstrous vampire Lauka Vai leads her undead hordes against the living, forever compelled – as are all her immortal breed – to gorge upon fresh and vital blood.

THE MIDNIGHT ARISTOCRACY

Beneath the pallid yet strangely beguiling appearance of a Soulblight vampire lies an inhuman terror that forever lusts after the taste of blood. Impossibly strong and preternaturally skilled in necromantic sorceries, they lead their resurrected legions against the living, fighting a relentless war in service to their monstrous hunger.

To face the armies raised by the Soulblight Gravelords is to battle against inevitability itself. No other force in the Mortal Realms illustrates the fate that awaits all life so starkly as these hosts of the risen dead. Hollow eye sockets aglow with baleflame, their warriors lurch across the battlefield in a grisly danse macabre, a mass of rotting flesh and clattering bones that swamps the enemy. No mortal, regardless of how courageous they may be, can deny the icy spear of terror that spikes into their gut as their cadaverous foes close in.

Sickness does not blight these corpse-armies; fatigue does not weigh at their limbs. They feel neither cold nor pain nor fear, for the vestigial flickers of awareness granted unto them extend only to the impetus to kill. At the will of their masters, they throw themselves against the shields and fortresses behind which the living cower, grinding them down through tireless attrition before turning rusted blades infused with potent ending-magics upon their foes.

Perhaps, a cunning soul may reckon, one could destroy those selfsame masters, ending the horror of the undead by disrupting the magic that animates them – but such is far easier said than done. These are the eponymous Soulblight Gravelords, a brood of vampiric warlords who have entered into the annals of infamy across the Mortal Realms. The curse that has claimed these unhallowed beings grants them strength, speed and resilience beyond the ken of any mortal; a vampire can burst from stillness to animation swifter than a man can blink, slaughtering a band of Chaos Warriors or mob of hulking orruks with nothing but their claws and sharpened fangs.

Yet physical power is not the only boon offered to the vampires; indeed, many possess an unearthly charm. The true nobles of undeath, these are no hissing ghouls or wailing wraiths, though their cold beauty and dark charisma is all too often a veneer beneath which their monstrous true nature lurks. They are immortal, and even on the rare occasion that one is 'slain', they are nigh on impossible to truly destroy – and they will inevitably return to wreak their vengeance. The sinister beasts of the night are theirs to command and are capable of spreading the curse to those whom they deem worthy, propagating the terror of the vampires until it has sunk deep into lands and empires far and wide.

Most terrible of all, many Soulblight vampires are potent reservoirs of necromantic energy and are capable of harnessing this power for sinister purposes. The battlefields of the realms have been fought over countless times across the bloody centuries, and beneath the surface lie shallow graves and corpse pits containing the remains of warriors who met a violent end. With the aid of their necromantic acolytes, a vampire can resurrect such legions on a grand scale, calling them forth from these gravesites to do battle. Yellowed bones and rotten flesh are infused with hellish vigour as the dead rise, clawing aside the topsoil at their master's compulsion.

But it is not only ancient corpses that are susceptible to necromancy: the bodies of those slain battling the dead are soon added to their morbid armies, falling upon their former comrades with a slack-jawed and mindless ferocity. This is the true horror of the Gravelords, and one in which many vampires find cruel amusement, for if it is dreadful enough to face the armies of lost ages, how harrowing must it be to battle against the puppeteered corpses of those who were allies and loved ones mere hours before?

Though proud Soulblight vampires typically wield their armies with the same disdain an unsentimental carpenter does their tools, there is an undeniable morbid majesty to these resurrected hosts. Ranks of skeletal warriors stand to attention, rusted spears held high and banners snapping in an ethereal wind. Wights clad in verdigrised armour or mounted atop unliving destriers charge alongside sneering vampiric cavaliers, their horns sounding out an unearthly dirge. Packs of undead wolves prowl at the army's flanks, hunting for stragglers, while flights of bats ranging in size from smaller than a man's fist to bigger than a warhorse circle and shriek through the midnight skies above.

It is the vampires themselves who ought to be feared the most, however. Whether fighting on foot or from astride hulking corpse-behemoths, they are capable of cleaving through scores of lesser warriors with contemptuous ease, directing the advance of the undead through will alone. Even in the midst of battle, they will take the time to feed on their enemies, draining their blood in vitae-drenched slaughtering sprees. In doing so, they acknowledge – if only for the briefest of moments – the cursed monster that lurks within them all, that ravening beast that threatens to slip free if afforded even the slightest opportunity.

THE HORROR OF THE VAMPIRE

Vampires are not natural creatures. They are an aberration, a form of twisted unlife whose origins ultimately stem from the matchless ambition of one being – Nagash.

It was Nagash's peerless necromantic knowledge that was harnessed in ancient times by Neferata – then an ambitious mortal queen – to create the first vampires. However, as with all things born of the Undying King's magics, there was a price to be paid. Those mortals who plundered Nagash's nine unholy books for the secrets of immortality did indeed find what they sought, but they were cursed in return for all their new-found power, forced to feed upon fresh blood for sustenance or else wither away to a final, bleak oblivion. From the grandest undead lords of Shyish to those emaciated beings that stalk the crystal catacombs of Hysh, all vampires wrestle with a constant desire to sup upon the blood of their former kindred – an ever-present hunger that, in almost every case, eventually comes to overwhelm them.

Not all those afflicted by the Soulblight curse are inherently evil. Hidden throughout the societies of the Mortal Realms are unfortunates who fight to control their bloodthirst while maintaining a pretence of normality. Even in places where vampires reign openly, most notably the Innerlands of Shyish, some have shown themselves to possess the capacity for compassion, honour – even love. But such examples are a rarity. The majority, those who truly own the title of Gravelord, see the living as nothing more than sweet delicacies to be gorged upon at their leisure.

These vampires style themselves as imperious wolves stalking amongst flocks of mewling livestock, feasting as they will. Part of this tendency towards malignance no doubt stems from the bestial hunger lurking within each vampire, a curse that will one day turn them into a soulless monster no matter how virtuous or noble they may once have been. Just as likely, however, is the notion that those mortals chosen to receive the blood kiss – the mysterious ritual through which a Soulblight noble creates another of their brood – often share the wicked natures of their sires. From ominous keeps surrounded by crimson moats, they plot to subjugate new lands, expanding their grave-empires and feasting upon the mortal inhabitants in bloodthirsty bacchanals. For vampires, the lust for domination is all – another trait no doubt acquired from the Great Necromancer.

So long as they ultimately obey, Nagash cares little for the machinations of individual vampires. Though their capacity for independent thought can render them fractious, it also ensures the Soulblight dynasts number amongst his most cunning and creative of generals – and should he need to remind them who holds the power, a flexing of his will can subdue even the Mortarchs, however grudgingly.

There are just as many vampires who chafe under Nagash's rule as do honour him, but even these acknowledge the relative freedoms granted to them within the dictates of their god's necrotopian ideal. Be it playing the parts of immortal kings and empresses, honing their battlecraft to heights beyond any mortal, or simply indulging their bottomless thirst for blood, the motivations of the Gravelords are as diverse as the vampires themselves. When the undead rise from their graves, all should tremble with fear, for with them they bring the promise of an endless night, one in which mortals are no more than servile thralls destined to provide gory sustenance to their immortal betters.

'Of the Knights of the Briar was Sir Traion, valiant defender of the Everqueen's groves. Against the drake-ogor king of Neos, he battled. Into the gut of the plaguebeast Guttoroch, he drove his thrice-blessed lance. But when Traion and his kin rode against the Lady of Cursewood, they were to be undone. No mortal queen was this – she was of the Nevergreen, the Redsap Feasters, the Dhampyre Brood.

Vampire.

To her was owed tribute of blood, paid by the men of Cursewood Vale, and five barrow-kings of Neos were her hand. Against her demesne did the Briar Knights ride, yet one by one they met their ends. A hundred dead men did Sir Konrek fell, yet a hundred more did drag him down. Upon Sir Bythorn did the lupine revenants of the deep woods prey.

At last, Traion stood alone. Through the halls of her castle of withered oak did he stride, There to behold a ghastly sight. Above the broken body of the Grand Master, the Lady of Cursewood stood. Down her pale chin, his blood ran. In her sanguine eyes, the beast raged.

Brave Sir Traion drew his blade, and yet the fiend did merely smile. From the shadows marched a parade of corpses, the remains of Traion's kin. Soon, the Lady said, he would serve at her pleasure for all eternity – a reward for his valiance.

Thus did the Knights of the Briar close in, and Sir Traion prepared for his final battle...'

- An excerpt from the 'Chronicles of the Midnight Equinox', a collection of folk tales gathered from the Reclaimed of the Everspring Swathe.

'Our enemies are but a flock of frightened, mewling sheep. We are the wolves. Ours is the right to prey upon them as we desire, for are we not the most majestic of the Undying King's creations? Summon the legions. Wake our warriors from their charnel pits. The hunt begins now.'

THE UNDYING KING

The history of the Soulblight vampires is intrinsically linked with that of their creator, Nagash, the Great Necromancer. This sinister avatar of undeath has stalked the cosmos since time immemorial, and from him the curse of necromancy has spread far indeed.

Few recall the origins of he who would become the Supreme Lord of the Undead. Even as a mere mortal in the World-that-Was, Nagash possessed boundless ambition. Using forbidden lore extracted from the ancestors of the aelves, he became the father of necromancy – the sinister sorcerous art through which the dead may be raised. Over the centuries, Nagash rose and fell several times, but always his machinations brought great strife to the living. As his mastery of necromantic magic increased, his powers rose to the brink of godhood.

Though Nagash's physical form was sundered in the destruction of the World-that-Was, so skilled in death magic was he that his essence had become joined to that of Shyish. When that bleak realm coalesced into being, so too did the Great Necromancer. At first, Nagash was trapped beneath a vast realmstone cairn, the sheer magical density of the piled grave-sand enough to suppress even him – a property he never forgot. For decades, he could only rage against his confines, until salvation came from an unexpected source.

Sigmar and Nagash were not strangers. In a past life, they had warred against one another, the God-King striking down the Great Necromancer. But Sigmar viewed his mission to bring civilisation to the realms as above all other concerns; protean, primordial god-things stalked Shyish in those times, and if Sigmar was to match their power, he would have to seek alliance with a being of their ilk. Better to lean upon the devil one knew. After much deliberation, he freed Nagash. In turn, the Great Necromancer grudgingly agreed to join the Pantheon of Order, for he has always been possessed of a strange sense of justice. Even then, however, Nagash plotted for the day he would rise to claim sole dominion of the realms.

Nagash soon set about conquering Shyish, bolstering his own power as his tireless undead minions assisted in the construction of new cities for the living. Many other death deities held sway over the underworlds, but over the centuries, almost all were consumed by Nagash; only Morrda, Master of the Bleak Raven, worshipped in the city of Lethis, is rumoured by some to have escaped. As Nagash cemented himself as the one true god of Shyish, he set to work constructing his citadel, Nagashizzar, at the realm's heart. From this necropolis-city, illuminated by lambent clouds of tortured spirit-essences and so redolent in death magics that sheer proximity to it could wither a mortal to dust, Nagash ruled. He accepted the worship of the living even as he secretly dispatched Arkhan the Black – most trusted of his servants – and his Deathrattle legions to begin moving vast quantities of grave-sand from the realm's edge to its centre in preparation for a grand ritual of ending.

It was at this time that the first vampires of the Mortal Realms came – or, more accurately, were summoned – into being. Three they were, each a champion of the World-that-Was: Neferata, Mannfred von Carstein and Ushoran. Nagash scoured the underworlds in search of their fragmented soul-essence, binding it into physical form so they could serve him once again. Though Ushoran was to fall from favour and succumb to his own strange curse, the former two proved worthy of claiming the mantle of Mortarch, standing amongst Nagash's inner circle of warlords.

Yet even such an exalted position could not sate the proud vampires' ambitions. Bitter rivals of old, Mannfred and Neferata sought to undermine one another, and since the Age of Myth, both have schemed to free themselves from Nagash's control. In spite of this, they aided loyally – if grudgingly – in the conquest of Shyish, and those underworlds they claimed as their own soon grew to reflect their new masters. Castle Sternieste and the palace-city of Nulahmia became infamous throughout the realms, macabre testaments to the glory of Nagash's deathless elite.

Mannfred and Neferata were to sire a new generation of vampires in the Mortal Realms, granting the blood kiss to those who most impressed them with their ruthlessness and guile. These early new-bloods could claim to be von Carsteins and Nulahmians for true. They fought as generals and champions in the mighty legions of the Mortarchs, serving as their sires' hands and agents even as they sought advancement for themselves. As the vampires spread across the Eight Realms and adapted to new homelands, however, they gradually became more distinct in terms of culture, heraldry and appearance. Before long, vampires could be found from Chamon to Ghyran, and each undead lineage was known by its own curious traditions and idiosyncratic curses.

The vampires ruled as provincial barons and satraps in Nagash's empire, a line largely unbroken to this day. In ancient times, all but the most bloodthirsty maintained an uneasy alliance with the living – though they were never fully trusted – and their ability to raise up vast undead armies in short order left them well disposed to fend off rampaging greenskin warclans or beastman Greatfrays. All the while, Nagash moved closer towards his secret aim of snuffing out all life and bringing his unchanging necrotopia to fruition. Given enough time, he may have accomplished just that, but behind the veil of reality, other powers conspired to bring about an end of their own…

THE BATTLE FOR SOULS

Nagash does not suffer theft lightly, least of all when it involves the precious souls that are the basis of his power. Such is his megalomania that he would see all of creation suffer for these crimes, with the perpetrators – Sigmar, the Ruinous Powers, the aelven gods and more besides – punished most harshly.

Shyish held out longer against Chaos than some realms. Nagash's focus was squarely upon his prime domain, and he was not one to acknowledge the possibility of defeat. As the Barrow Wars began and the underworlds were ravaged by hordes of daemons, both living and dead inhabitants of the realm battled the invaders. Foremost amongst the resistance were the vampires. They had invested too much in their grave-empires to lose them, and their immortal cunning and vast undead armies were an undeniable impediment to the Chaos advance. Mannfred's Legion of Night launched ambush after ambush against the attackers, while from her capital of Nulahmia, Neferata puppeteered a network of agents and assassins to keep abreast of the foe's movements before unleashing her own Legion of Blood in decisive counter-strikes. Though the hordes of ruin attacked relentlessly, none could say that Shyish was not well defended.

Yet though they won many a battle, the sheer momentum of the daemon legions saw the Gravelords gradually lose the war. Part of this was down to the vampires themselves, for even in such a crisis, many could not bear to relinquish their authority and submit to any outside of the Mortarchs, who could not be everywhere at once. Sigmar's rage also worked against Nagash. The God-King was furious that the Great Necromancer did not look to the defence of realms beyond his own; when promised undead aid did not arrive to support the Azyrite legions defending the Endgate, Shyish's arcway to the Allpoints, Sigmar's temper broke. He pursued Nagash across the underworlds, annihilating armies that could have been used to stall the daemons. At the Battle of Black Skies, the collapse began in earnest. In his citadel, Nagash was cut down by Archaon the Everchosen, and only a desperate push by the Mortarchs prevented his utter destruction. With Nagash's power sundered, Shyish was easy prey. As underworld after underworld fell to the daemons and Nagashizzar was sacked, the vampires had little choice but to retreat into the shadows, husbanding their strength and striking out when possible.

Sequestered in the underworld of Stygxx, Nagash slowly recuperated. As he did so, he remained aware of what transpired in the wider realms – and was outraged. Not only were the souls of those mortals who pledged themselves to the Dark Gods sucked into the Realm of Chaos upon their demise, but from Azyr, accursed Sigmar was snatching away worthy warriors on the brink of death. This was transgression enough, but when Nagash realised that the God-King was also ransacking the underworlds in search of mighty spirits, an eternal vendetta was sworn. He named Sigmar thief and traitor, for he believed their former alliance was built upon the premise that all dead souls would pass to Shyish. Revenge was inevitable.

A STORM OF DEATH

When Sigmar's Tempest surged across the realms, Nagash knew it was time for his return. He burst through the Starless Gates and set upon the Chaos forces, the Mortarchs at his side. Gales of amethyst magic howled across Shyish, resurrecting the dead on a mass scale and drawing the Soulblight nobles from their lairs. Many of these vampiric warlords soon rallied to the side of their master, joining the march on occupied Nagashizzar. That bleak metropolis was soon reconquered, the eight fortresses of black iron built around it cast into ruin and the bodies of those Chaos Lords charged with custodianship crucified upon its osseous walls, their souls cursed to burn in baleflame for eternity. Such was the price of insulting Nagash.

For a time, Nagash lurked in his fastness, taking little part in the Realmgate Wars. Even as the first free cities rose, he did not stir. But this inaction was a ruse. Arkhan the Black continued his mission to accumulate vast quantities of grave-sand, and little by little, that realmstone was refashioned into black pyramids that were suspended point down in the skies around Nagashizzar. The greatest of these was positioned right above the city, and it was this that Nagash intended to use as the crux of his sinister ritual.

By the time the other powers became aware of Nagash's machinations, it was too late to halt them. Only the interference of the skaven saw the grand spell of realm-spanning demise go awry. The results were still horrific. The Necroquake, a cataclysm of Shyishan magic unlike any that had gone before, erupted across the cosmos and shook them to their foundations. Deathrattle legions and Deathwalker hordes numbering in the thousands were wrenched from shallow graves to march across the lands with no greater purpose than to bedevil the living.

THE SOUL WARS

Nagash's spell did not simply see the dead rise in numbers uncountable – it fundamentally rewrote the magical laws of Shyish. The Great Black Pyramid became so infused with death energies that it sank into the very bedrock of the land. With the greatest source of aetheric energy now at the realm's heart rather than at its edge, Shyish buckled. The sinking pyramid contorted the realmcrust and formed the yawning abyss known as the Shyish Nadir, at the bottom of which lay Nagashizzar, now so saturated with morbid power that even the Great Necromancer could not remain there indefinitely. The Shyish Nadir not only drew in souls as a whirlpool did ships but also threatened the underworlds themselves: every continent was being slowly but inexorably dragged towards the maw of the black void, there to be devoured and used to strengthen Nagash. As hopelessness set in across an underworld, its drift towards the Nadir would accelerate. Nagash was quick to capitalise on this, and his undead armies fought to break the will of those mortals in the Amethyst Realm as much as they did to conquer, speeding up the process by which the underworlds and the souls therein would become one in him.

For the Gravelords, the Soul Wars that followed were a time of bloody plenty. They were given licence to spread doom and misery amongst the living as they willed, free from the shackles of grudging alliance or a common enemy. From the Mortarchs' legions to the merest of dynasties, every vampiric lineage saw an opportunity to claim glory. Entire regions were ravaged, while morbid sepulchres and cairns redolent with deathly energies were raised over mass graves. The ascension of the Mortarchs Olynder and Katakros stirred unease amongst the old order and compelled them to prove their worth all the more aggressively. Bastions of Order, Chaos and Destruction were besieged by hosts of unquiet spirits, with even the dreaded Eightpoints being breached. Every mortal that fell replenished the ranks of the Gravelords – and such fresh corpses were not in short supply, owing both to the cataclysmic battles taking place and to the wild, lingering magics unleashed by Nagash's gambit.

Nagash's greed, however, was to betray him. Seeking to expand his power to other realms, he charged Arkhan, Mannfred and Neferata with working evil rituals around realmgates connected to Shyish, collapsing them to form soul-sucking lesser nadirs. The armies of the dead marched in force, bringing untold suffering as the Mortarchs went about their work. Yet, ultimately, they were to be defeated. Mannfred's ambition was to play a role in this: deliberately matching himself against overwhelming odds, he took the chance to flee and launch an annexation of Neferata's unprotected lands. Arkhan was to open a lesser nadir in Ymetrica, most mountainous of Hysh's nations, but the liche was repelled by the gleaming hosts of the Lumineth. Seeing this, Nagash sought to triumph personally where his Mortarch had failed. Though he nearly succeeded in snuffing out the spirit of Mount Avalenor, greatest of Ymetrica's majestic peaks, he was sundered at the last by the will of Teclis and his allies, giving the Mage God a chance to work a grand counter-spell to drain the Necroquake of its fury.

The Soul Wars had ended, but the lines between the living and the dead had been irrevocably drawn. Glutted upon their successes, the Soulblight Gravelords saw no reason to halt the conquering advance of their barrow-armies.

THE PERFIDY OF THE AELVES

Sigmar's crimes were most heinous to Nagash, but he was not the only one to earn the god's ire. The Great Necromancer had long suspected that the aelven deities were extracting a glut of stolen souls from some hidden source, and the appearance of new aelven peoples only cemented his beliefs. Some, such as the Idoneth Deepkin, even compounded the blasphemy of their creation by stealing away the essence of other mortals to serve their own fey purposes. When an Idoneth enclave was discovered on the bed of Shyish's Khaphtar Sea, Nagash knew that he had found more foes who sought to thieve from him – and who had to be punished accordingly.

Perhaps not all this antagonism stemmed from a twisted sense of law. Even when the Pantheon of Order flourished, Nagash's towering ego had often butted against that of another god – Archmage Teclis. Both were the greatest wielders of the arcane, and neither took well to the notion of having an equal, let alone a superior. Every exchange carried with it a bladed word, each deity probing the temper of the other. Indeed, the unexpected unleashing of the Necroquake served as a statement of intent by Nagash to become the ultimate mystic power in the cosmos. Conflict was, in all likelihood, always inevitable.

THE REALM OF DEATH

Often portrayed as a land of barren moors, crumbling mausoleums and seemingly endless graveyards, Shyish is the most morbid of all the realms. Here, mortals have long attempted to coexist with the dead, yet the works of Nagash threaten to unravel all this.

Shyish is the end made manifest. All the Mortal Realms are formed from compressed magic, but the Realm of Death is unique; the underworlds, as its bleak continents are known, are each fashioned from the mythical concept of an afterlife as held by cultures throughout the realms. As such a belief grows more widespread, aetheric energy will coalesce into a new underworld at the realm's edge. In time, that underworld will come to be populated by the departed souls of those whose belief gave it form. Many Ghurish tribes perceived the afterlife to be an eternal paradise of battle and feasting, and thus after death they came to dwell in Hallost, the Land of Dead Heroes. The people of Ossia, meanwhile, lived lives of such toil that even death was no end to their labours, and their underworld is a place of exertion in which honest work is its own reward.

Yet Shyish is not a realm populated by the dead alone – as much as some of those departed souls may wish otherwise. Since the Age of Myth, mortal civilisations have risen throughout the underworlds, forging an existence in their unforgiving lands. The greatest concentration of these was once found in the Prime Innerlands, those underworlds closest to the heart of Shyish and thus furthest from the Perimeter Inimical. Nagash's grand ritual of inversion has, however, imperilled these cities and nations and threatens to see them dragged into the hungering maw of the Shyish Nadir, there to be broken down and transfigured into pure amethyst energy. As hopelessness and despair set in across an underworld, its drifting progress towards the Shyish Nadir accelerates. None exemplifies this better than the isle of Szargorond, where stands the cursed city of Ulfenkarn – domain of the cruel wolf-lords of the Vyrkos Dynasty – that now all but dangles over the precipice of oblivion.

The Gravelords fight a tireless war against trespassers to their domain. Even in places where the living have not been butchered wholesale, atrocity is commonplace. The tomb-city of Gharnost is perpetually shrouded in gloom and ruled by Deathrattle monarchs known as the Blind Pentad. Gharnost pays its tithes to Mannfred von Carstein by supplying his armies with fresh bodies, and the despairing inhabitants have learnt to dread the ominous rattle of the Corpse Carts that prowl the fog-swathed streets.

Then there are those places that are a testament to the price of defying Nagash. In the deserts of Penultima stands the corpse of Shadespire, a once thriving city whose Katophrane rulers uncovered the means of preserving their souls after death through the use of a mystical material known as shadeglass. The Great Necromancer, who has always proven miserly with the souls he considers his rightful property, did not take kindly to this affront, and so he cursed the city. Shadespire was twisted through space and time until a shadowy reflection of city – and the souls forever trapped within – was transported to the twilit sub-realm of Uhl-Gysh. Those who venture to

the ruins of Old Shadespire in search of shadeglass may find themselves passing into the Mirrored City and sharing in its time-broken curse, doomed to fight and fall over and over again in an unbreakable cycle of death and resurrection. None escape.

Mannfred von Carstein's legacy is writ large in the underworld of Carstinia. It is a land of creeping forests and cloying bogs where artefacts torn from a thousand conquered nations lie scattered beside ill-maintained dirt roads. Oppressed peasantry mark their doors with symbols of warding and rarely stray far from the villages in which they were born, for horrors prowl the misty marshes and sinister woodlands: packs of slavering Dire Wolves, shambling Deadwalker hordes and worse things besides. In truth, Mannfred cannot abide to remain in Carstinia for long, as it is but a mocking echo of past glories he never truly achieved – a cruel jest on Nagash's part. He spends little time ruling from the grim fastness of Castle Sternieste, instead leaving his vampiric offspring to squabble amongst themselves as he pursues his own agenda.

Neferata, by contrast, has expended much time in fashioning her citadel of Nulahmia into a crown jewel of Nagash's necrotopia. Though the city has come under attack several times, it has never once fallen. Many are its grim wonders: the Pathway of Punishment, a wide switchback road around the colossal Throne-Mount lined with grotesque and constantly operational torture devices; the Grand Chapel of Night's Hunger; and, of course, the Palace of Blood itself.

The inner sanctums of Neferata's palace are luxuriously decorated, as befitting a true Soulblight queen. Gilded statues of animal-headed gods remembered by none save the Mortarch stand guard outside temple-cloisters in which gory rituals of bloodletting are performed each night. Neferata's chosen courtiers – vampires one and all – prowl the alabaster corridors like jackals on the hunt, eternally practising their talent for intrigue on one another and vying for the favour of their regal mistress.

GRAVE-SAND

Grave-sand is the realmstone of Shyish, a fine black particulate of solidified death magic. Each grain is connected to a single life and can be manipulated by those with sufficient arcane skill to affect the thread of that creature's mortality. Grave-sand has long been regarded as a potent tool of necromancy; vitrified gems of the substance are prized items in a Necromancer's arsenal, while vast quantities were used by Nagash to create his black pyramids and power his grand spell of ending. Vampires who seek mastery of the sorcerous arts will go to great lengths to acquire grave-sand artefacts, for the power over life and death that they provide can be used to wither living foes in moments or keep undead armies constantly animated.

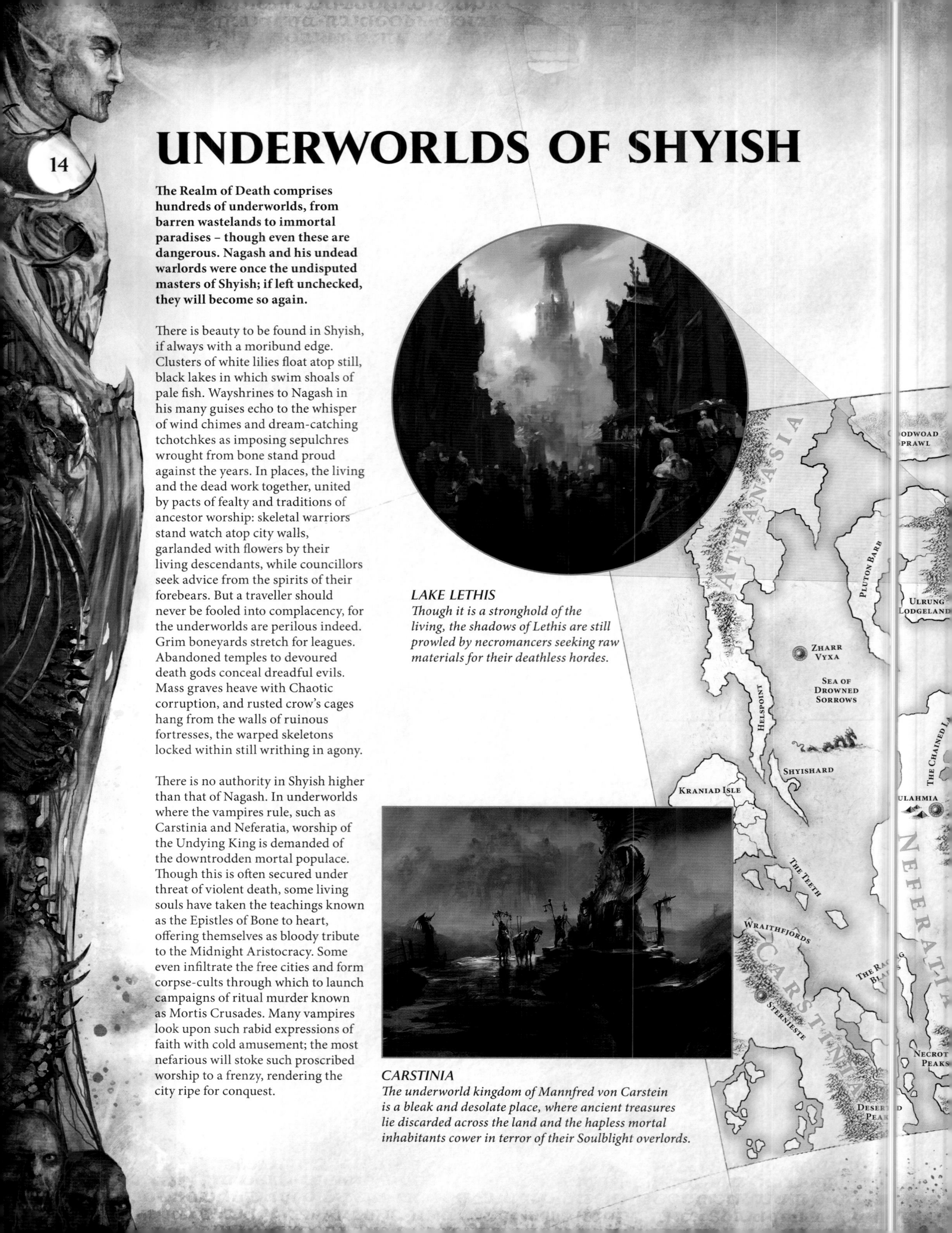

UNDERWORLDS OF SHYISH

The Realm of Death comprises hundreds of underworlds, from barren wastelands to immortal paradises – though even these are dangerous. Nagash and his undead warlords were once the undisputed masters of Shyish; if left unchecked, they will become so again.

There is beauty to be found in Shyish, if always with a moribund edge. Clusters of white lilies float atop still, black lakes in which swim shoals of pale fish. Wayshrines to Nagash in his many guises echo to the whisper of wind chimes and dream-catching tchotchkes as imposing sepulchres wrought from bone stand proud against the years. In places, the living and the dead work together, united by pacts of fealty and traditions of ancestor worship: skeletal warriors stand watch atop city walls, garlanded with flowers by their living descendants, while councillors seek advice from the spirits of their forebears. But a traveller should never be fooled into complacency, for the underworlds are perilous indeed. Grim boneyards stretch for leagues. Abandoned temples to devoured death gods conceal dreadful evils. Mass graves heave with Chaotic corruption, and rusted crow's cages hang from the walls of ruinous fortresses, the warped skeletons locked within still writhing in agony.

There is no authority in Shyish higher than that of Nagash. In underworlds where the vampires rule, such as Carstinia and Neferatia, worship of the Undying King is demanded of the downtrodden mortal populace. Though this is often secured under threat of violent death, some living souls have taken the teachings known as the Epistles of Bone to heart, offering themselves as bloody tribute to the Midnight Aristocracy. Some even infiltrate the free cities and form corpse-cults through which to launch campaigns of ritual murder known as Mortis Crusades. Many vampires look upon such rabid expressions of faith with cold amusement; the most nefarious will stoke such proscribed worship to a frenzy, rendering the city ripe for conquest.

LAKE LETHIS
Though it is a stronghold of the living, the shadows of Lethis are still prowled by necromancers seeking raw materials for their deathless hordes.

CARSTINIA
The underworld kingdom of Mannfred von Carstein is a bleak and desolate place, where ancient treasures lie discarded across the land and the hapless mortal inhabitants cower in terror of their Soulblight overlords.

THE PRIME INNERLANDS

THE PRECIPICE OF DOOM
The Shyish Nadir relentlessly draws underworlds towards its hungering maw. The Cursed City of Ulfenkarn now stands upon the very precipice of annihilation.

GOTHIZZAR
The morbid fortress of Gothizzar surrounds the Endgate and has been the site of many desperate struggles between the servants of Chaos and Nagash.

LORDS OF THE NIGHT

The vampires have spread far across the Mortal Realms. In every land beyond Azyr, there are those who bear the Soulblight curse and lead legions of the risen dead to accomplish their dire aims. But vampires do not spring wholesale from the aether, and over the centuries, a complex web of lineage and bloodlines has come to connect them all in unlife.

Every vampire ultimately descends from the dark triad of Neferata, Mannfred and Ushoran. While Ushoran's brood were to degenerate into the delusional abhorrant cannibal kings, those sired by the Mortarchs came to exemplify the pale and refined image of a vampiric aristocrat. However, the independent nature of the vampires and the highly divergent cultures from which they were drawn led to many of them forging their own paths. As they travelled new lands and developed new obsessions with which to while away eternity, the magics of the Eight Realms also began to alter the curse that raged within them; though the constant blood-hunger remained, some found the bestial aspects of their personality sharpened, their command of necromancy intensified, or even stranger alterations besides. Thus were the dynasties born, each an unhallowed lineage ruling in the dark places of the realms.

Few vampires would deny the primacy of Mannfred and Neferata. The Mortarchs are creatures of immortal cunning and malice, their existence spanning millennia. Numbering amongst Nagash's foremost generals, both have been placed in command of vast undead armies known as legions. Numberless hordes of shambling corpse-warriors and prowling beasts of the grave fill out the ranks of these hosts, and in the Mortarchs' absence – for they cannot be everywhere at once – vampiric majordomos and lordlings are charged with carrying out their masters' agendas. The most trusted of these either are sired directly by the legion's overlord or hail from client dynasties that have proved themselves loyal and capable servants. On occasion, a Mortarch may take direct control of a lesser dynasty's forces, usually to exploit their idiosyncratic skills in war or to make an undeniable gesture of dominance. Rarely are they refused, for only Nagash stands higher in the hierarchy of unlife than they. Still, the Mortarchs often allow the masters of a dynasty to retain nominal joint command, the better to cement alliances or, with the Mortarch pulling the strings from the shadows, manipulate lesser lordlings.

Beneath the legions stand innumerable dynasties. Each stems from a single vampire patriarch or matriarch whose particular curse permeates their brood. Some dynasties are tight-knit clans where the blood kiss may only be granted by the express permission of the dynastic head; others – often those of an unstable nature – seek to sire as many potential offspring as possible in the hope that some will resist the frenzied beast within.

Like the noble houses of the free cities, each dynasty possesses its own traditions, heraldry, bitter rivalries and scurrilous gossip. Many such characteristics are defined by the magical curse within them reacting to the inherent energies of their home realm as much as any cultural or sociological factor; for instance, Aqshian vampires struggle to control their raging passions and thus spread their line as far as possible, while the withered Tengorez of Hysh emerge only rarely from their crystal lairs in order to capture the arcane war machines of the Xintilian armies and corrupt them to better focus necromantic energy.

Though they cannot rival the legions, the greatest dynasties are rightly infamous. Some lord it over conquered grave-empires, while others follow their bloodlust wherever it leads. Few exemplify this better than the Wraith Fleet of Varkos Varactyr, whose army of drowned mariners and rotting titans of the deep sails across the Mordacious Sound to menace the southern coasts of the Great Parch.

In addition to the undead hordes summoned forth from scattered gravesites across the realms, vampires are often escorted by courts of attendants, warlords and sycophants. The skeletal remains of ancient chieftains and monarchs, Wight Kings call on Deathrattle warriors from ancient battlefields and barrows to serve their will. Their tactical prowess remains sharp, and they are often entrusted with acting as frontline champions for the Gravelord armies. Though the lowliest Wight Kings are susceptible to a vampire's sorcerous control, the greatest are possessed of a will equal to any of Nagash's blood-sucking aristocracy; these rule their own deathless empires and send their subordinates to treat with vampiric rulers of stature. Necromancers, meanwhile, are Deathmages offered a less glorious but just as vital role: to ensure that the undying armies remain filled with morbid vigour and to resurrect those who fall. Wise vampires offer patronage to as many promising Necromancers as they can, for doing so allows them to focus on slaughtering the foe and sating their dark thirsts.

THE HIERARCHY OF DEMISE

Nagash's ultimate desire is to create a necrotopia of deathless stasis with him as its ultimate master. Below the Great Necromancer stand his legions, vast armies commanded by Nagash's Mortarch lieutenants that, in the cases of the Legions of Night and Blood, contain vampires drawn from the Soulblight dynasties. Some dynasties are entirely supplicant to a singular legion, while others are locked in a state of subtle or overt civil war as different vampires seek to chart different paths for their bloodlines. The greatest dynasties, such as the Vyrkos, Kastelai and Avengorii, are held in almost as much dreadful awe as the legions themselves. Though they are largely disregarded by prideful Nagash until their aims align with his own, the greatest dynasties – much like the parasitic creatures that fill their ranks – grow stronger by feasting on their kindred, unleashing their undead hordes to subsume their lesser rivals and forming complex webs of allegiance that see the mightiest matriarchs and patriarchs wield power to match that of any living emperor.

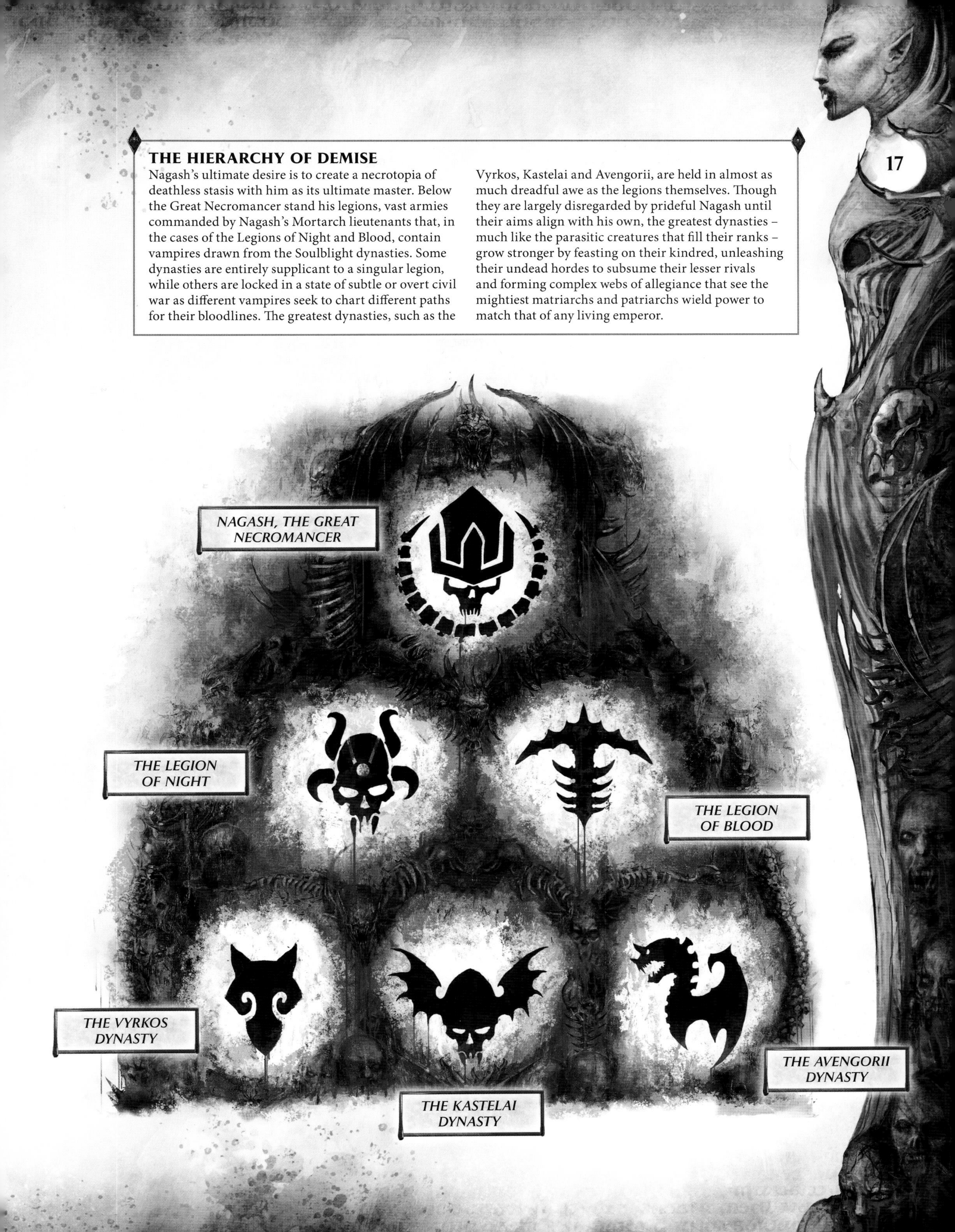

LEGION OF NIGHT

Ruled by the cunning Mannfred von Carstein, the Legion of Night is perhaps the most infamous of all Gravelord hosts. These resurrected armies assail the living in a seemingly endless tide, driven on by the impetus of their masters and drowning the foe in a surge of mouldering bodies.

Mannfred von Carstein has always been defined by his towering ambition. The colossal legion bound to his will is a testament to this. No vampire controls as much raw military strength as he does, and the Mortarch would gladly send thousands of his minions into the grinding press of war to achieve his hate-fuelled designs. This disdainful pragmatism is common to many rulers of the undead, shorn of the morals of the living as they are, but few exemplify it better than von Carstein and his disciples. Those vampires who serve the Mortarch of Night are amongst the cruellest and most callous of their breed; they consider themselves the true lords of the night, far above the mortal chattel they oppress and feed upon with such cold relish. Any undead noble who displays even the slightest hint of reservation is soon disposed of and replaced by one who cleaves more closely to the ideals of Soulblight supremacy.

The von Carsteins are an ancient lineage, and of them Mannfred is the most venerable and most to be feared. He has seen entire ages pass and kingdoms beyond count flourish and decline, and he has come to appreciate a defining truth: no one is invincible or irreplaceable. Even a god can fall – Nagash himself proved that much when he was broken by the Everchosen. In this, the proud vampire sees opportunity. After millennia of servitude, Mannfred remains determined to one day escape the Great Necromancer's clutches and become the sole overlord of death. This aspiration is not purely a product of his arrogance; Mannfred knows the Great Necromancer well enough to consider what would happen should the necrotopia ever be realised and the blood-gorging terror of the vampire no longer be needed to cow the living.

Though few true von Carsteins remain – having been slain by brave heroes at great cost, descended into blood-crazed lunacy, cast off their heritage to form new lineages or been betrayed to their destruction by the jealous Mannfred – many of the dynasties sired by the Mortarch's blood-spawn still pledge obeisance to the Sanguine Throne of Carstinia. Mannfred's legion does not lack for capable generals, and many a grave-empire across the realms is ruled by a vampire granted dominion over conquered lands in return for their undying loyalty. For the most part, Mannfred is content to allow his subordinates to pursue their own desires so long as they bring misery to the living, though when he himself rides at the head of his armies, he suffers nothing less than total obedience.

The Legion of Night is a truly vast entity. Even Mannfred himself likely does not know for certain the number of vampires and vassal dynasties that have been compelled, cajoled or otherwise forced into his service over the centuries. Behind each of his subservient Soulblight lords shamble great hosts of the undead bound to the will of the vampires. Mannfred is not discriminatory when it comes to those corpses necromantically drafted into his armies. Some of his vampiric generals, particularly the more martial-minded fiends, clad their minions in midnight-black cloth as a sign of fealty. Others lead armies still bearing the colours they did in life, and it is not uncommon to see detachments of the Legion of Night with many different faded hues amongst their lines. Masses of moaning Deadwalkers, their ranks comprising everything from pitiable lepers to pampered nobles, lurch forward as a tide of rotting flesh and fabric, while Deathrattle cohorts march in eerie lockstep beneath washed-out banners stitched with the symbols of long-forgotten empires.

Though all vampires will raise reinforcements from shallow graves or the piled bodies of the freshly slain in the midst of battle, few do so with the dispassionate efficiency of those sworn to the Legion of Night. Mannfred's creed – that honour, morality and notions of prideful dignity are nothing more than impediments to victory – has been eagerly seized upon by his disciples, for they see no reason to consider anything save their own selfish desires. Huge swarms of moaning Deadwalker Zombies and clattering Deathrattle Skeletons are ripped from their resting places without hesitation and directed at the foe. With a relentless, unthinking determination, they advance into storms of arrow fire or onto waiting blades, shrugging off what would be mortal injuries as their sheer weight of numbers overwhelms the foe.

While his hordes of risen dead may be mindless, Mannfred himself is anything but. Long centuries of vying for ultimate dominion have made him the master of the conniving ploy and the dishonourable act. There is no stratagem the Mortarch will not employ in pursuit of his goals.

Resurrecting waves of pox-ridden zombies to spread wasting disease; working lingering torture upon captives within the walls of their own cities before brutally executing them and reanimating their mutilated bodies; forming temporary, false alliances with desperate mortal commanders only to seed their ranks with vampirism: Mannfred has enacted all of these ruses in the past and more besides. His ability to swiftly assess and exploit the changing circumstances of any battlefront makes him an incredibly versatile tactician, and this has proved to be the cornerstone of his many triumphs. Though the preening courtiers of Nulahmia may consider his methods woefully crass and the warrior-lords of the Kastelai decry him as an honourless cur, the Mortarch of Night cares not a jot. He is long in the fang enough to know that power and victory are the only true measures of success – a sentiment that appeals to the Great Necromancer, even if Nagash would never admit as much in Mannfred's presence.

Tales of Mannfred's conniving ways are recounted from the towers of the Varanspire to the halls of High Sigmaron. Many Soulblight nobles within the Legion of Night seek to emulate their master and earn his favour through the greatest displays of ingenuity and cunning. Those who succeed are kept close as part of von Carstein's inner circle of warlords – largely so he may keep an eye upon those who prove too clever for their own good – but the lord of Carstinia is wise enough to see value in all manner of servants. The fealty of particularly brutish vampires and, more recently, the twisted monstrosities known as Vengorian Lords is accepted by the Mortarch as regularly as the fidelity of those of a more subtle nature; after all, even a crude weapon can prove deadly if wielded with sufficient skill.

Once, the Legion of Night served as Nagash's foremost terror weapon. Such was disputed by the ascension of Lady Olynder and her Legion of Grief, but Mannfred's long-honed ability to profit from rapidly changing circumstances has ensured that, rather than lose his place in the undying order, he is now more vital than ever to the Great Necromancer. There is no military conundrum he cannot crack, no apparent misfortune he cannot turn into a boon. When Arkhan the Black butchered his retinue of Necromancers, the Black Disciples, to create a cabal of powerful Ossiarch Mortisans, the vampire gladly offered patronage to the scattered survivors, ensuring that he would possess a host of talented Deathmages – and, more importantly, the knowledge of those who studied under his rival Mortarch – to keep his armies marching.

Mannfred was one of the undead champions chosen by Nagash to spearhead the War of the Mortarchs. Together with Neferata and Arkhan the Black, he was to extend the hunger of the Shyish Nadir across the realms. Of course, the vampire was far from a perfectly loyal servant. When his efforts to create a lesser nadir in Invidia were repulsed, von Carstein was quick to retreat to Shyish, wasting no time in leading his hosts to annex Neferata's unprotected borderlands while the Nulahmian queen was engaged on her own mission.

Mannfred von Carstein is a wild card who can be trusted only to be untrustworthy, but in his unpredictable nature, Nagash sees a valuable asset that will forever keep his enemies off kilter. His endless hordes march against the living with a tireless vigour, and when alloyed with the cruel cunning of this most spiteful of Mortarchs, there is no foe on either side of the grave that they cannot defeat.

THE BATTLE OF ROTSOUL MIRE

Few battles exemplify Mannfred's genius better than the one fought at Rotsoul Mire. Here, the Mortarch's armies slaughtered the Flyblown Legion – a contagium of Rotbringers who had spread their Grandfather's noxious gifts across many an underworld – to the last man. Other undead generals had attempted to engage the Nurglites on more favourable ground, only to be overcome by the Rotbringers' pox-blessed weapons. Mannfred took a different tack, presenting the glory-seeking champions of Nurgle with an irresistible opportunity: to slay a Mortarch on marshy ground that favoured their warriors. Mannfred, however, knew the terrain well from centuries of rulership; beneath Rotsoul Mire was a hidden realmgate to Aqshy through which bright magic ebbed and flowed, periodically turning the swamp into a boiling sludge. As the Flyblown Legion pursued the apparently fleeing Mortarch, they were suddenly set upon by hordes of zombies emerging from beneath the stagnant surface, their flesh already too blackened to harbour new strains of infection. Even as they were dragged down by scores of grasping hands and began to boil in their rusted armour, the veteran Rotbringers still had the best of the fighting – but Mannfred was not finished. The mountains ringing Rotsoul Mire were the hunting grounds of Vargheist packs that Mannfred permitted to feast in his domain in return for their allegiance. They rallied to his call now, falling upon the rear of the Flyblown Legion in a storm of tearing fangs and leathery wings. Mannfred himself rode at their head, annihilating the Grand Rot-Provost Festerbelch in a storm of aetheric death energies – to slay such a champion ingloriously from afar well suited the Mortarch's spiteful temperament.

LEGION OF BLOOD

The Legion of Blood is a force replete with contradiction: a weapon of subtlety and grandeur alike, equally skilled in the employment of patient intrigue and of lethal force. Such is entirely fitting for the army of the Mortarch Neferata and the macabre aristocracy she has crafted in her image.

The Legion of Blood is the splendour of the Midnight Aristocracy unleashed, the epitome of many vampires' vision for the realms. Ranks of bleached skeletal warriors stand to attention while darkly beautiful vampiric nobles stride at their fore, striking down hapless mortals with cold and biting laughter. Yet behind the image it presents upon the battlefield, the legion is a nebulous thing, its goals and machinations as inscrutable as they are effective. Truly, then, it can be said to reflect the will of she who rules from the centre of its sanguine web – Neferata, Mortarch of Blood.

Neferata is an ancient creature who thrives on disaster and dominion. While most undead are naturally drawn to stagnation, she revels in overcoming the mutability of circumstance; the secret libraries of Nulahmia are filled with treatises penned in drained vitae by the vampiric monarch expounding her learnings on mastering the shifting eddies of power. A being of depthless cunning with a well-honed talent for intrigue, Neferata epitomises the side of the Soulblight curse that drives a vampire to seek mastery over all things. In Neferatia, the underworld she has claimed as her own, many peasant villages are little more than blood farms where living chattel are broken in will, butchered and served upon the feasting tables of Nulahmia's undead aristocracy. The mortals native to that illusion-shrouded city – and such do exist, for Neferata desires command over both the living and the dead – fare little better. Through ancient traditions such as the Culling of the Firstborn, the Feast of Morbheg and the Dance of the Red Goblet, she keeps the noble houses suppressed and at one another's throats while identifying candidates to 'bless' with the blood kiss. Neferata's favour is typically bestowed upon females, though not to the point of exclusivity – any who display a penchant for command, intrigue and subtlety are ripe for induction into the blood of Nulahmia. Many of these newly sired vampires are ordered to sate their thirst with the blood of their own kin, binding them to Neferata in evil and removing potential rebellious thorns from the Blood Queen's side.

It is the duty of Neferata and her most trusted courtiers to serve as Nagash's spymasters and agents of anarchy. Across the long millennia of her existence, the Mortarch has refined the principles of manipulation into a veritable art form. From the opulent inner sanctums of the Palace of Blood, she weaves a web of corruption so vast and staggering in its complexity that none save Neferata herself have any hope of truly comprehending it. Few are the mortal-held territories that do not play host to secretive blood-cults, vampiric covens and underground societies of Necromancers sponsored by the lords and ladies of Nulahmia.

A savant of espionage, Neferata employs an extensive repertoire of techniques to direct her agents in accordance with her will. Many of these are mystical in nature, such as scrying fonts filled with the fresh, glistening blood of sacrificed seers and ensorcelled Fell Bats that roost in crumbling mausoleums and serve as her eyes; nevertheless, the Mortarch retains an appreciation for handwritten correspondence. Her keen mind is capable of processing and retaining information from hundreds of sources simultaneously, while her decrees are immaculately inked upon parchment wrought from the flayed flesh of nobles and scented with luxurious Nulahmian perfumes.

Neferata has expended a great deal of effort in establishing one of the finest spy networks in all the Mortal Realms. There is no almost secret that can be concealed from her should she desire to unmask it; while Mannfred and his brood may be renowned for their ability to find opportunity amidst adversity, the Mortarch of Blood maintains that only by turning a foe's misfortune into a weapon can true victory be achieved. Her devoted servants see into the war camps of the Eightpoints, the guildhouses of Kharadron sky-ports and the mansions of magnates throughout the free cities. The Clearblood Fellowship, a sub-branch of the Order of Azyr dedicated to unravelling Neferata's network of watchers and agents, even harbours quiet concerns that she has successfully planted her most skilled intelligencers into Azyrheim itself – though how such a masterstroke may have been achieved remains the subject of intense speculation.

The overlords of the Legion of Blood value many kinds of information but prize military intelligence above all. Though not as openly contemptuous of the living as their counterparts in the Legion of Night, these self-proclaimed aristocrats revel in any opportunity to outfox and outmanoeuvre 'lackwit' mortals before annihilating them on the field of battle. Tireless undead armies will march for days on end to seize sites of strategic worth or arcane power, fortifying them before expeditions of living soldiery can even finish mustering. Enemy commanders of note will be investigated and appropriate counter-hexes devised. Expert vampiric saboteurs will wield potent ending-magics to spoil an army's rations or summon illusory mists to waylay marching columns. By the time a rival force finally encounters the Legion of Blood in all its terrible majesty, their defeat will already have been orchestrated down to the smallest detail. All that remains is for the vampire covens entrusted with generalship to ensure that their mistress's designs are carried out to perfection. The terrifying splendour of these undead nobles clad in full war regalia is a potent weapon in itself.

The core of the Legion of Blood is composed of Deathrattle barrow-cohorts. While Neferata and her favoured generals – the Sanguinarchs and Vampire Lords of Nulahmia – will resurrect hordes of the more-freshly slain when necessity demands it, they consider Deadwalkers to be unsightly servants, unbefitting of those who value the finer things in unlife. Clad in polished armour and cloth dyed shades of scarlet and imperial purple, ranks of skeletons form an imposing wall of bleached bone. Rather than simply grind the foe down through mindless attrition, however, these cohorts will engage key portions of the enemy line before parting their ranks to allow lances of Black Knights and retinues of Grave Guard to deliver the killing blow.

Forearmed by their extensive spycraft and the experience they have garnered over the span of many lifetimes, the commanders of the legion often seem to know what tactic will be employed against them before the enemy themselves do, arranging their fleshless minions to expertly counter the enemy's ploys. These vampiric courtiers lead their hosts with such precision that even Katakros the Undefeated has been known to offer a solitary nod upon witnessing them in battle – high praise indeed from the fabled Mortarch of the Necropolis.

Neferata's armies are grand affairs despite their macabre nature. Her skeletal servants are resplendent in death, their bones cleansed with scented oils or painted with fine inks; in Nulahmia, there exists an underclass of mortal slaves charged with ensuring the legion's cohorts remain immaculate – on pain of becoming a meal for the vampires. Many of the legion's elite wights were once members of Nulahmian noble houses, their armour and banners still bearing their former heraldry. Though there is perhaps an element of queenly vanity in this pageantry – no doubt intensified following the rise of the darkly glorious Ossiarch Bonereapers – as with everything the Mortarch of Blood does, strategy remains paramount. Neferata knows the power of perception; though she may not send her hosts into battle as readily as some of her kin, when she does give the order, it is always to make a definitive statement of strength. Those who face the Legion of Blood are confronted by a terrifying yet bleakly majestic enemy that seems to know their every move in advance, and despite the aristocratic airs to which they cling, the vampires who hold command take satisfaction in tearing apart foes with a bloodthirsty zeal.

THE COURT OF NULAHMIA

Nulahmia is one of the great vampiric capitals of the realms, and thus it is unsurprising that so many bearing the Soulblight curse make it their lair. Many come seeking the personal favour of Neferata, offering their terrifyingly effective combat prowess for the Queen to wield at her discretion. These vampiric warlords and knights are amongst the most skilled in all the realms, perhaps rivalled only by the bladelords of the Kastelai Dynasty – a fact that weighs bitterly on both sides. There are also those vampires who were sired by the masters of Nulahmia and who have spent many mortal lifetimes enjoying the luxuries of Neferata's court. All but the most bestial of vampires can detect the subtle differences between blood derived from varying sources, sampling it as a sommelier would a casket of fine Ghyranite wines, but Nulahmians are particularly refined in this field; the city hosts a great many of the consumption-obsessed Sanguinarchs, who view the battlefield as a chance to blend gory flavours spiced with warlike emotion. The courtiers of Nulahmia are not so far removed from their mortal lives that they do not still scheme for power, however. The gilded halls of the Palace of Blood are as much a hotbed for skulduggery and scandal as any mortal equivalent. Still, Neferata tolerates this only insomuch that it does not interfere with her greater aims.

While most Gravelord armies may have one or two vampires at their head, those hailing from the Legion of Blood tend to be commanded by entire covens. Particular courtiers will be assembled and dispatched by Neferata to oversee her complex schemes, ensuring that their ambitions play against one another. Whether riding upon enchanted divans and palanquins or soaring atop majestic undead drakes, these vampires fight as a lethal concentration of force that revels in the chance to satiate their gory hunger.

VYRKOS DYNASTY

Animalistic and strange, the Vyrkos are among the most infamous of all Soulblight dynasties. Though they may affect a refined-if-rugged persona, playing the part of warrior-kings and nobles, the truth is far more savage: behind their thick furs and cold expressions, the Vyrkos are little more than ravening beasts who would turn the realms into their stalking grounds.

The Vyrkos were born of the dark, freezing forests of Shyish. Here, ashen-barked and black-leaved trees grow close and tall, and the ground is covered in dense banks of snow – as well as the frozen bodies of those who met their ends amidst the grim woodlands. Despite the frosty chill that forever lingers on the air, few of these unfortunates perished through simple cold; those not torn apart by savage wolf packs or the other slavering predators that roam the forests are instead found violently exsanguinated, their faces drawn in a rictus of terror. Wanderers who chance upon such sights would be wise to turn back, for should they press on further, they will enter the territory of the Vyrkos Dynasty. In those frozen lands, only death awaits.

The Vyrkos refer to themselves as the Blood of the Wolf. Like many dynasties, they possess their own unique strain of the Soulblight curse, but theirs is a near-uniquely bestial manifestation. Scraps of ancient Shyishan legend tell that the first of the Vyrkos, Belladamma Volga, was not sired by any vampire but instead created upon bargaining with the undead godbeast Hrunspuul, the Hound of the Cairns. In return for his gifts, the spiteful Hrunspuul cursed all of Belladamma's line to reflect the qualities of one of the many totemic animal-spirits venerated in their strange tribal culture, of which the wolf was most sacred. Some scholars of matters vampiric believe that the shape-changing abilities commonly attributed to all Soulblight creatures in folklore throughout the realms derive from witnessing Vyrkos vampires on the prowl. Many granted the blood kiss by a Vyrkos vampire are swiftly overwhelmed by this curse, reduced to a bestial state not too dissimilar to that of the hated abhorrants. More venerable Vyrkos have learnt to control their animal core, but they cannot suppress it entirely – nor do they try. The rarely seen Elders of the Vyrkos are said to be as much wolf as they are undying prince, and those who restrain their bestial selves behind a courtly facade inevitably become all the more monstrous when their true nature is unleashed.

Though they employ cruel pack tactics in battle and revel in the thrill of the chase, the Vyrkos are not simple butchers and brutes. They strive to maintain balance between their human and bestial personas, employing each when it is most appropriate. Though nomadic by nature, for the urge to hunt the living pounds through their minds like a tribal drumbeat, they are no less besotted with conquest than any other vampire. On several occasions, Vyrkos lords have laid claim to permanent holdings, of which the cursed Shyishan city of Ulfenkarn is by far the most infamous. These vampires will raise up armies of the dead and assemble courts of undying lieutenants and functionaries, and many can play the part of the aristocratic Soulblight noble convincingly – if, in the case of true 'wolf-bloods', with a particularly savage and warlike edge. Yet one should never be fooled into believing that the beast within is quiescent. The Vyrkos are blood-hungry terrors through and through, a fact reflected in every aspect of their lordship. Their halls are stalked by slavering Dire Wolves, their kingdoms are haunted by those vampires who could not master their transformations, and the cold sneers worn by the Vyrkos nobility are but brittle masks concealing the monsters that coil within their souls.

THE CURSED CITY

The Vyrkos have staked a claim in many lands throughout the realms, but the cursed city of Ulfenkarn is their grandest achievement. It is a vision of what awaits should the Soulblight Gravelords triumph, where vampires gorge upon terrified mortals even as their lands are overwhelmed by the raw energies of death.

Ulfenkarn is a city lingering on the precipice of annihilation. Once the proudest bastion of civilisation to be found on the Shyishan isle of Szargorond, it has been beaten down by years of bloodshed, tyranny and arcane onslaught until any glory it could be said to retain is only of the most sinister bent. Macabre spires and palaces grasp towards the faded sky, while the corpse-gardens of the city seem to have spread almost with a mind of their own, making it difficult to tell where they end and the rest of Ulfenkarn begins. In the shadows of these ghoulish sepulchres and mausoleums, mortals trudge beneath the vigilant gaze of skeletal watchmen, their minds numbed by years of despair and oppression. Even during the day, the primacy of the dead in Ulfenkarn is undeniable, but it is at night that the true horror of existence in the city becomes apparent. The living cower in their hovels and bolt their doors tight, knowing that anyone found on the cobbled streets after dusk will soon become prey for the Vyrkos vampires, they who feast upon the carcass of the city that is Ulfenkarn.

Ulfenkarn, once known as Mournhold, was plunged into darkness by the dreaded Vyrkos lord Radukar the Wolf. The vampire and his minions twisted the very soul of the city until it became both a hunting ground to satisfy their animalistic thirsts and a grisly tribute to their undying glory. Statues of the Wolf rose over dilapidated quarters and thoroughfares, and it was said that the vampire king could detect even a thought of sedition and punish transgressors appropriately. Ghoulishly, there is more truth to this than outsiders reckon: vermin are often utilised by those Vyrkos whose curse is more rodent-like in nature to spy on potential troublemakers. The Vyrkos brood revelled in the oppressive atmosphere forced upon their subjects, and none more so than Radukar and his Thirsting Court of sycophants and underlings. The Wolf knew full well that the hopelessness he imposed upon Ulfenkarn ensured that all of Szargorond would gradually be drawn towards the maw of the Shyish Nadir – and he was correct, for the city now stands practically at the lip of that devouring void. This proximity to the source of the Necroquake saw his powers swell as never before, thus proving – in Radukar's own mind, at least – the superiority of the immortal Vyrkos over the craven living.

Though Ulfenkarn has become infamaous as the stronghold of the Vyrkos, Radukar did not initially come to the city as a conqueror – quite the opposite, in fact. During the Age of Chaos, the city of Mournhold was poised to fall to a very different foe: the Khornate warhorde of the Daemon Prince Slaughn the Ravener. Doubtless the city would have been taken by the Blood God's hordes, had it not been for a fleet of dark-hulled vessels sighted upon the horizon, sails emblazoned with the sigil of a snarling wolf's head. This fleet belonged to Radukar, and he and his veteran army of ogor mercenaries, whom he had recruited from the freezing underworld of Kosarg, fell upon the Khornate army with a savage fury, scattering the warhorde to the chilling winds. In the aftermath, the Grand Princes of Mournhold had little choice but to accept Radukar as one of their own – they certainly did not have the military strength to deny the vampire's demand, as much as they knew it was a hellish bargain. For a time, however, Radukar seemed content to play the part of the noble lord. The blood kiss was, on the surface, granted to other aristocrats of Mournhold but rarely, and the vampire and his ogor minions enabled the city to hold out even through the dark years of the dominion of Chaos.

But this was all an act to disguise Radukar's true intent. Guided by the shamanistic Elders of the Vyrkos, the Wolf had learnt of tangled prophecies speaking of a deathstorm that would one day ravage Shyish, and it was foretold that Mournhold would be positioned near the very eye of that morbid tempest. Sure enough, when the Necroquake howled across the Prime Innerlands, Radukar was well placed to gorge on its arcane fury. Aided by traitors within the ranks of Mournhold's nobility and the savage Blood-born he had sired, the Wolf made his play for dominance. Hundreds of the city's living denizens were slaughtered to perform grand rituals of ending, while others were dragged away to the grim Ebon Citadel – Radukar's stronghold since his arrival – to meet a grisly end. Those who remained were forced into subservience by prowling vampires, marching cohorts of skeletal watchmen, moaning packs of Deadwalkers, and the Kosargi Nightguard – Radukar's ogor elite, now passed beyond the veil of mortality and rendered all the more unstoppable for it. Worse still, Torgillius, the Wolf's chamberlain, had perfected the creation of vile artefacts known as grave-sand phylacteries; these ensured that even should Radukar and his inner circle be struck down, they would soon return once more – albeit by using the Shyishan realmstone to steal the

soul of an unwitting victim. With his power cemented and the city itself warping as gales of death magic blew through the streets, Radukar renamed his conquest Ulfenkarn – 'the Wolf's Feast' in the harsh tongue of the Vyrkos.

But even in this grim age, there were heroes to be found – those who were determined to prevent Ulfenkarn from sliding into blood and madness. Liberated from the dungeons beneath the Ebon Citadel, a group of champions came together to oppose the Wolf. It was their intent to kindle a flame of hope within the downtrodden citizens of Ulfenkarn, a flame that would one day erupt into a rebellious inferno. Operating out of the Kharadron blockade runner known as the *Adamant*, the ragtag alliance of the living struck out against Radukar; they reclaimed ancient treasures, toppled blood fonts and crafted deadly realmstone weapons capable of opposing the vampires. Through their courage and conviction, they were even able to infiltrate the Ebon Citadel and deal Radukar a mortal wound. The Wolf was forced to flee, though unbeknownst to most, he is far from slain.

Now, a small but growing haven of the living has been established in Ulfenkarn. Though it is a ramshackle thing, as riddled with corruption and vice as any free city, it is nevertheless hoped that from this crude seed, the Mournhold of old will one day rise again. Yet matters are never so simple in Shyish. Many powerful Vyrkos nobles still hold sway in Ulfenkarn and now battle for control of the city even as they seek to destroy their mortal adversaries. Worse still, Radukar – his animal rage now unchained – prowls relentlessly through the shadows. Those he chances across are brutally torn apart, their remains strewn gorily across their streets for their fellows to find. So far, all efforts to hunt the transfigured Radukar have ended in disaster. How much of the vampire's mind remains is difficult to tell, though he undoubtedly seeks to revenge himself, both on the heroes who defeated him and the city that now defies his monstrous will.

KASTELAI DYNASTY

The Kastelai are a lineage of vampiric warriors obsessed with martial prowess. Riding out from the ominous, translocating fortress known as the Crimson Keep, their mounted hosts plunge into the most terrible battles imaginable as they dedicate themselves to perfecting the art of bloody hand-to-hand combat.

No vampires are as martial-minded as the Kastelai. War is their defining obsession: testing themselves against the most worthy of foes is considered the only honourable way to spend their eternal existence. Indeed, the Kastelai make a great show of their supposed honour. As they would have it, their commitment to open battle grants them a nobility rarely found among the undead , for they channel their dark hungers into honest contests of arms. It is certainly true that the sight of their massed mounted echelons clad in their gleaming plate and clutching pennants that snap in the freezing wind is glorious in its own morbid fashion. One should never be fooled, however; though they may style themselves as dark paragons of the battlefield, the Kastelai are just as prone to succumbing to the predatory madness that is the Soulblight curse as any other vampire lineage. In war, they find an excuse to let their most vile and bloodthirsty excesses reign.

Outsiders are often perplexed by the many legends surrounding the Kastelai. Some tales describe them as nomadic undead warriors, while others name them the Castellans of the Crimson Keep. Contradictory as it may seem, both these claims are true. The Crimson Keep is no simple fortress: it is a supernatural terror from the darkest Shyishan myths, a sinister apparition drawn like some ghoulish bone-jackal to feast upon reservoirs of death magic. It is difficult to predict where the Crimson Keep will manifest, but it always does so amidst the ruins of tumbledown castles and broken fortresses. As the sky overhead darkens and swirling clouds of bats fill the night air, the stones of these fallen citadels will run like wax, transmuting into stark walls and twisted minarets the colour of fresh gore. From out of the yawning portcullis-mouth of the Keep, the Kastelai emerge to trample cities and smash into the flanks of unprepared armies – so besotted with war and carnage are they that any knightly honour they possess is only of the most warped variety.

At the head of the Kastelai rides Prince Vhordrai, the Saint of Slaughter and Fist of Nagash. Though bound to the Crimson Keep as a punishment for his past transgressions against Nagash, Vhordrai is all but venerated by the Kastelai, many of whom were granted the blood kiss after managing to unseat one of his undead warriors in a joust. On the rare occasions where Vhordrai does not lead, a senior Soulblight warlord – often one of the Red Seneschals, Vhordrai's feared inner circle – will take command, ruling with an iron fist and maintaining their vaunted rank through the greatest displays of combat prowess.

Unlike in more close-knit dynasties, a vampire does not have to be sired by one of the Kastelai to join their ranks. Any who swear themselves to Prince Vhordrai and pass the excruciating martial trials set before them may become one of them. These 'adopted' vampires bring with them combat traditions drawn from a thousand heritages, which are then refined by their new brethren.

The Kastelai take intense pride in furthering their understanding of warfare, and they see no better way to spend eternity than by pushing the craft of battle to its utmost limits. On the rarest of occasions, a Kastelai vampire will even spare a worthy living adversary in exchange for being taught some new technique or philosophy of combat that has caught their attention. The multifarious origins of the Kastelai not only facilitate a wide breadth of combat skills but also the sharing of beliefs from many militant cultures. In the winding halls and shadowed alcoves of the Crimson Keep, cults of battle worship at secret altars dedicated to the most warlike death gods, drawn from societies across the realms. These sects are suffered to exist by Prince Vhordrai only so long as these orders remain quiet, for though the Saint of Slaughter despises Nagash, he is not fool enough to draw the Great Necromancer's wrath twice.

Kastelai armies are often almost entirely mounted affairs; this not only maintains their knightly image but is also born of necessity, for with each bloody dawn, the Crimson Keep relocates and any vampires left behind are either stranded or, should they have spent too long within its halls, cursed to wither away entirely. Lances of Blood Knights form the core of their forces, supported by Dire Wolf hunting hounds raised from the most ferocious canine beasts. Kastelai vampires will resurrect slain infantry from local barrows and corpse pits if need be, but these soldiers are considered entirely expendable and left to crumble as dawn's light breaks across the sky. The Kastelai strike hard and fast, whether offering their skills as mercenaries to other dynasties – always for a heavy price in blood – or riding out in force to impress their own brand of violent oppression upon the living.

AVENGORII DYNASTY

As warped in mind as they are twisted in body, the Avengorii are a clan of monsters and nightmares. Their savagery is infamous even throughout the predatory lands of Ghur; those few foes courageous enough to meet them in battle are inevitably gorily torn apart and consumed to feed their bestial hunger.

Merely to look upon the hosts of the Avengorii Dynasty is to risk being driven mad with terror. These Ghurish vampires have long since abandoned even the pretence of humanity; having surrendered to the raging beast within and supped deeply upon powerful ending-magics, the dynasts are now true terrors of the dark. Accompanied by flights of shrieking Vargheists and bloated corpse-monsters who swoop down from the shadowed skies to tear at the foe, these warped Gravelords give full rein to their unnatural impulses, feasting upon clotted gore and spreading utter desolation as their savage whims dictate.

Unlike the Vyrkos, the Avengorii make no effort to restrain their monstrous aspect. The majority are not generals, knights or connoisseurs but ravening abominations who believe the beast within ought be embraced. Even their abodes, located deep beneath the dunes of the Sascathran Desert, are unlike any other Soulblight keep. Under the amber sands lie vast honeycomb chambers with gnarled fortresses that cling like stalactites to the cavern roofs. None know who first fashioned these bizarre fastnesses, but they have long since been claimed by the Avengorii. The malformed Soulblight beast-kings known as Vengorian Lords prowl the darkened corridors, while echoing vaults serve as lairs for the many zombified drakes and chiropteran horrors drawn to the fell aura of the Avengorii. When war calls, these beasts claw their way to the surface through ancient, winding tunnels, led by Vengorians who seek to demonstrate the primacy of their bestial forms over lesser beings.

Though there is an undeniable comparison to be drawn, the Avengorii are a breed apart from the abhorrants of Ushoran – indeed, they take great offence at the comparison, as more than one mortal has discovered to their cost. The lords of the Sascathran Dunes are generally lucid, if not sane, and the majority are well aware of how ghastly they appear to others. Many Avengorii make a show of revelling in this apparent disgust, though such may simply be a way of coping with the transformation they have wrought unto themselves. Either way, through acknowledging their own primal natures, they have proven more than capable of thriving in the savage lands of Ghur.

The Avengorii have developed many strange rituals intended to feed their monstrous nature. The *mas'ranga* sees an untransformed vampire – a despised underclass amongst the Avengorii – willingly bound in iron chains and suspended over a pool of boiling blood, their thirst for gore stoked to such a frenzy that it rapidly accelerates their transmutation into a Vargheist. During the *korak'hor*, a vampire must spend ten days and ten nights in isolated meditation before the Void Maw, a realmgate within the greatest of the suspended fastnesses that belches forth great waves of amethyst energy and is rumoured to be linked to Nagashizzar itself. After the tenth night, the chamber is unsealed; in most cases, the vampire will have been reduced to dust by the intensity of death magic they have endured, but some succeed in 'ascending' as a Vengorian Lord. Though other vampires look upon the Avengorii's practices with bewilderment and disdain, the lords of the dynasty are too deranged to care. In their minds, their trials are holy acts and enduring them will see them achieve true communion with their so-called 'curse'.

Avengorii armies are, in truth, almost undeserving of the name. While there are some Wight Kings – the remains of proud nomad-chiefs who roamed the Sascathran Desert in life – who see it as an honour to lead their Deathrattle hordes to battle in the shadow of the Avengorii, their forces are little more than packs of bloated vampiric predators accompanied by towering beasts of the grave. They fall upon the foe without hesitation, ripping them apart in an orgy of bloodthirst and violence. For the majority of the Nightmare Brood, strategy is forever relegated to a distant secondary status when offered the chance to feed their lust for bestial carnage. If left unchecked, the Avengorii would likely burn themselves out in a conflagration of omnicidal hunger, yet a chance for salvation flickers in she who rules them: Lauka Vai, the Mother of Nightmares.

Once a vampiric knight possessing a firm code of honour, Vai has retained a sense of nobility despite her transformation into a hideous Vengorian. She considers feasting upon the blood of defenceless mortals as being beneath true Soulblight warriors and instead directs her apostles towards the great beasts of Ghur and other, more worthy prey. Though there are those Avengorii who slip the leash, they have found foes in the rampaging hosts of Chaos and Destruction upon whom they may unleash their full, bestial fury.

CHRONICLES OF ENDLESS NIGHT

Since time immemorial, the Soulblight Gravelords have preyed upon the peoples of the realms. Their undead armies have brought suffering and misery to thousands over the long centuries, and the vampires will not cease until every mortal kingdom has been ground into meek subservience beneath their lifeless heels.

AGE OF MYTH

FIRST OF THE BLOOD

The Mortarchs Mannfred and Neferata are resurrected by Nagash and, in turn, sire the first vampires native to the Mortal Realms. They spread first across Shyish and then far beyond, ruling over many lands and establishing their undying dynasties. The lifeless hordes at their command prove well suited to repelling rampaging beasts of the wild as well as intimidating mortals into submission.

THE WAR OF THE NAIL

In the Chamonic lands of Gazan Zhar, the duardin Jurgermok clan is outraged when the High King's daughter is slain. The murder weapon – a long iron nail – is found near the scene branded with the sigil of the Gorgaz clan. Though joined by distant ancestry, competition over mining rights has soured relations between the clans. When apparent retaliatory attacks slay the prince of the Gorgaz, a bitter grudge war begins. Any who attempt to halt the conflict disappear in night ambushes or marches through the oily swamps.

After decades, the battered remnants of both clans meet amidst the mountain tombs of their ancestors to make peace. It is then that the true orchestrator, Mannfred von Carstein, strikes. Emerging from a realmgate deep below the tombs, the Mortarch takes a cruel satisfaction in raising the bones of ancient duardin to fight for him. The Jurgermok and Gorgaz fight side by side against this outrage, but to no avail – Mannfred's legions grind them to nought, and much rune-lore concerning the passage of souls is offered in tribute to Nagashizzar by the triumphant von Carstein.

AGE OF CHAOS

THE BARROW WARS

The Age of Chaos begins in blood and madness. Legions of daemons pour through cracks in reality, slaughtering thousands and laying low entire kingdoms. The hosts of Khorne and Nurgle are particularly committed to conquering Shyish – the former would have the mightiest warrior-spirits bound to his bloody service, while the latter seeks to control the cycle of life and death. Undead and mortals alike strive to repel the armies of the Dark Gods, but even the tireless servants of the Gravelords are slowly pushed back.

RAGE OF THE GOD-KING

When Nagash fails to send promised aid to the Endgate in Gothizzar, Sigmar is outraged. Ignoring the wars raging elsewhere, the God-King pursues Nagash, smashing aside entire undead armies in his furious desire to hunt down the Great Necromancer. Several times do the rival gods meet, though Nagash escapes each time. At last Sigmar relents, but only after destroying and sealing away Katakros, Nagash's finest general, in the Midnight Tomb. All the while, the forces of Chaos have tightened their stranglehold on those underworlds still reeling from Sigmar's fury.

THE BATTLE OF BLACK SKIES

Archaon the Everchosen leads a grand host to the walls of Nagashizzar. The battle that follows is the stuff of legends: tens of thousands of daemons, corrupted mortals and undead warriors clash on the arid plains surrounding Nagash's fortress. Vampires duel with Chaos Lords, their blows too swift for mortal eyes to follow. Zombie Dragons clash with Greater Daemons, while Deathrattle shieldwalls break the charge of the infernal legions time and again. The Mortarchs stretch their power to the fullest, harnessing the energies channelled by Nagashizzar to wither entire portions of the battlefield.

At the centre of the conflagration, the Great Necromancer and the Everchosen duel. In such proximity to his own fortress, the Supreme Lord of the Undead is flush with arcane might, but Archaon in turn is bolstered by the direct favour of all of the Dark Powers, for to cast down a god is no simple feat. After a long and bitter battle, Archaon breaks Nagash asunder. Only a last-ditch effort by the Mortarchs saves their master from total destruction. The Great Necromancer's remains are stolen away to a hidden sepulchre and Nagashizzar itself is razed, the Everchosen himself installing those Chaos Lords who will garrison the ruins.

CURDLED BLOOD

Nagash plays no part in the Battle of Burning Skies, though some bands of honourbound Blood Knights do ride alongside their former allies in the pantheon. Despite ferocious resistance, Sigmar is forced to retreat to Azyr, and the tide of Chaos sweeps across the realms. Many Soulblight dynasties are wiped out, and even the Mortarchs are forced to retreat to their strongholds, repelling seemingly endless waves of aggressors.

COMING OF THE WOLF

The city of Mournhold is saved from annihilation at the hands of Khornate besiegers by the infamous Vyrkos lord Radukar the Wolf and his army of Kosargi ogors. The battle-weary inhabitants of the city resign themselves to subjugation, but Radukar is strangely merciful – all he desires is a seat amongst the noble houses of the city. Such is far from unheard of in Shyish, and in their desperation, the lords of Mournhold accept this devil's bargain. With a hunter's patience, Radukar and his minions spread the curse of undeath among the aristocracy of the city.

AGE OF SIGMAR

TEMPEST OF DEATH

As Sigmar's Tempest breaks, Nagash returns through the Starless Gates on a howling gale of death magic. Across Shyish, the dead rise en masse, and the vampires emerge from hiding to launch bloody crusades of retribution against the forces of Chaos. Nagashizzar is recaptured, and though he feigns considering a new alliance with Sigmar, in truth, the Great Necromancer recommences his plans to end all life in the realms.

A THORNED ROSE

Nagash remains largely quiet throughout the Season of War, but as the Time of Tribulations begins, a stirring from Shyish is detected. Many Lord-Veritants and agents of the Order of Azyr become increasingly obsessed with rooting out vampiric blood-cults nestled within the free cities, but for each coven purged, another two spring up. Behind many lurk Neferata and her handmaidens; taking advantage of their stretched-thin adversaries, they whisper in the ears of the powerful, compelling them to ignore those who warn of impending catastrophe and allow the graveyards of their cities to overflow their bounds. All the while, vampires of the Legion of Blood continue to infiltrate the cities of Sigmar, awaiting their Mortarch's command to take up arms.

THE BLOOD HUNT BEGINS

Though Nagash's scheme does not work flawlessly, the result is still devastating. The Necroquake howls across the cosmos, rewriting the laws of magic and causing the dead to rise up on an unimaginable scale. Now is the time of the Soulblight vampires' ascendancy as every civilisation comes under siege from these revenant armies and the Gravelords fighting at their head. Few places exemplify this better than Mournhold. Poised as it is near the very edge of the newly formed Shyish Nadir, the city is but a hair's breadth from being consumed entirely by that all-devouring maw, and Radukar and his minions soon take bloody control. Mournhold is renamed Ulfenkarn – 'the Wolf's Feast' – and the Vyrkos relish the chance to bring misery and suffering to its mortal inhabitants.

GLUTTED ON GORE

The Gorefang Mawtribe returns to their Glutthold amidst the Ruined Keeps of Asphyxia to feast upon the spoils of their raids. As their Butchers brew up great vats of blood, however, the fortresses begin to twist and morph. Even as the ogors let out furious howls of denial, the Crimson Keep manifests. From out of its gates, the Kastelai Dynasty rides in force, Prince Vhordrai at their fore. Blood Knights trample Gnoblar mobs without slowing to drive their weapons into ogor flesh, while the Fist of Nagash slays the Overtyrant Marg, spitting him on his Bloodlance before drowning him in the largest of the Mawpots. As the sun rises, the Kastelai retreat as swiftly as they came – though not before raising up a host of half-eaten zombies to drag as many Mawpots as possible into the Crimson Keep, their intent unknown as the fortress eerily disappears.

A HARVEST TOO FAR

The Bonereapers of the Ivory Host continue to impose their ghoulish tithes on conquered peoples along the Coast of Tusks. Upon arriving to collect from the fishing villages bordering the Krakensea, however, they are surprised to be opposed not by mortals but fellow undead – Lauka Vai and her host of Avengorii monsters. The Mother of Nightmares warns that the Ossiarchs disgrace their undead heritage, favouring simple and unworthy conquests rather than hunting the megafauna of Ghur.

A savage melee soon breaks out, bones crushed to powder or hacked apart with nadirite blades. Vai seeks out Ghuri-Xza, the Monarch of Tusks and liege of the Host. The two undead queens come to blows after Vai smashes aside Xza's Immortis Guard. Only the arrival of Vokmortian saves the Ossiarchs – the Master of the Bone-tithe agrees to impress upon the region only when the Ivory Host stands critically under-strength, while Vai pledges that there will be no further resistance from her brood. The Avengorii leave, but further down the coast, settlements find savaged and exsanguinated corpses washing up on their beaches with increasing regularity.

WAR OF THE MORTARCHS

Nagash charges Arkhan, Mannfred and Neferata with opening lesser nadirs across the realms to further Shyish's power at the cost of that of their adversaries. Thwarted by the forces of both Nurgle and Alarielle, upon retreating, Mannfred leads his armies not back to Carstinia but to Neferatia, annexing those regions left unprotected by the Mortarch of Blood. Enraged by both her own failure in Chamon and this latest transgression, Neferata calls upon her sycophants and bonded thralls to join her hosts. Even as the realms shake and fracture under a new age of war, open conflict between the two Mortarchs at last seems inevitable.

NAGASH, SUPREME LORD OF THE UNDEAD

Ancient and malicious, Nagash rules over Shyish as a tyrannical god. At his rasped command march seemingly endless armies of undead revenants, and by the power of his almighty sorceries have a thousand mortal empires been cast into ruin.

Nagash bestrides the realms as a morbid colossus, a terrifying and macabre deity who wields the energies of death as a mortal swordmaster does their blade. Levitating above the battlefield upon a storm of shrieking gheists, he is the end given form, the snuffing-out of the candle, the last grain of sand draining through the hourglass. All undead beings, from the lowliest Deadwalkers to the great Mortarchs, are his to command. To face him is to face ultimate oblivion, either through his intensely powerful magics or at the edge of the cursed blade Zefet-nebtar.

There is no being in all the realms who can rival Nagash's command of necromancy. Since pioneering that dark art, he has bonded with the energies of Shyish, and now his powers are seemingly limitless in scope. With a twitch of his bony fingers, he can tear loose the souls of a swathe of foes, violently exsanguinate them, sap them of all hope and vitality or – most dreaded of all – reduce even the mightiest adversaries to a pile of dust. Furthermore, Nagash's mere presence lends the armies of the risen dead a terrifying impetus. Such is his might that he can raise new undead warriors almost faster than an enemy can hope to strike them down, and when he focuses his will upon his servants, they are filled with a truly ghoulish vigour. Nagash takes malicious pleasure in unleashing these charnel hosts against the most favoured champions of his rival gods, unceremoniously dragging them down beneath a tide of bleached bones and rusted blades.

Nagash's panoply of war further displays his arcane prowess; by the Great Necromancer's own hand were these treasures crafted, and each serves to augment his already formidable might. Morikhane, the Black Armour, is capable of not only warding off attacks but redirecting them in a blast of ending-magic. Alakanash, the Staff of Power, is studded with gems of vitrified grave-sand that aid the channelling of Shyishan sorceries. Nagash's most prized relics, however, are the nine tomes of eldritch lore that hang from his cadaverous form on iron chains. Bound in cured human leather, the Nine Books of Nagash are the greatest trove of necromantic lore in all the realms; so thick is the aura of amethyst energy surrounding the volumes that merely standing near them can see a mortal age centuries in a matter of heartbeats. With these tomes, Nagash can muster a prodigious stream of incantations, his arcane dominance impossible to resist.

As many vampires hate and fear Nagash for his dominion over them as do worship him. When the Undying King calls, however, all Soulblight creatures are bound by instinctual compulsions to answer. In truth, Nagash often simply demands that their vast armies do his bidding, the service – and continued existence – of the vampires themselves permitted only so long as they are of use. Yet Nagash also recognises the value of those vampires who prove their worth. In the presence of the Supreme Lord of the Undead, these fiends are largely released from the need to constantly marshal their own hordes; instead, they are given full licence to destroy Nagash's enemies in as bloody and terrifying a fashion as possible.

Whenever the opportunity presented itself, which was rare indeed, Mannfred von Carstein travelled to the sepulchre-keep deep in the heart of Nagashizzar. Down here, at the heart of the Shyish Nadir, even a Mortarch could not exist for long. Knowing the Great Necromancer, he suspected that was the point.

But though it was physically unpleasant and served as a reminder of his own dismal Carstinian estates, Mannfred forced himself to come. He walked the echoing galleries, watching the luminescent sconces flicker with the light of agonised souls. A theatrical touch, but then given his long litany of achievements, one could forgive Nagash his occasional melodramas – and it brought Mannfred some satisfaction to know that the Lord of the Dead's claims of being beyond all passions and foibles were a manifest lie. Most regularly, the Mortarch came to the throne chamber set in one of the sepulchre's twisted minarets. He would linger there as long as possible, ignoring the ever-present tug of death magic at his very being as he stared up at the currently vacant throne. The vampire had never dared to ascend the winding staircase – fashioned from the ribs of some petty death avatar – to touch that godly seat. Even with it empty, he wasn't sure he'd survive the experience.

Ringing the hall were five shadeglass mirrors, each one framed by an ouroboros of bone limbs. Through such means did Nagash's court commune. Mannfred's own stood understandably vacant. Three others shared its inactivity. Katakros spoke little at their conclaves, his thoughts consumed by the Eightpoints offensive. As Mannfred reckoned it, the woefully single-minded Mortarch of the Necropolis could be entrusted to disregard virtually everything beyond that campaign, provided it did not sap his own resources.

Olynder… now, her next moves would be far more interesting. Though she was so often a maudlin weight around the neck – Mannfred had caught himself almost pitying that poor wretch Valentian, just the once – the vampire suspected the same ambition that had doomed the Veiled Lady in life had yet to be entirely snuffed out. After all, did Nagash not demand such things from his generals, even as he punished them for it?

Arkhan, meanwhile, would not be saying anything for some time, having been hurled from the rim of Hysh by the Lumineth. The Liche would return, of course; that was rather the point of him. Still, Mannfred would take great pleasure in reminding him of that inglorious episode.

The surface of the fifth mirror suddenly began to ripple like a font of liquid gore after a stone has been dropped into it. Scarlet light illuminated one half of Mannfred's pale features, warring with the pale green back-glow of the chamber. The vampire turned towards the mirror, dispelling the urge to draw Gheistvor even as he smiled. For a moment, he wondered how she had known he was here, before dismissing the notion. Of course she'd know. That was, to continue the prior thought, the point of her.

'Queen Neferata,' Mannfred sketched a lazy bow to the face resolving itself in the mirror. 'Are you cross?'

'I flayed Narazar today.'

'You're cross,' Mannfred chuckled. He held up his hands in mock apology as the Mortarch of Blood gave a wintery smile, her wine-red lips creasing in something that wasn't quite amusement. 'I had high hopes for Narazar.'

'Then you shouldn't have left him in charge of your flanking forces,' Neferata replied, as airily as if they were discussing some emergent Nulahmian fashion. 'Bold of you to quit the field after committing to annexing my lands.'

'You didn't seem to be doing anything with them.'

'Mannfred, Mannfred. Why do we have to keep having this conversation?' Neferata sighed as she shook her head, night-black hair spilling across her shoulders. She was still smiling. 'What do you think Nagash will do when he realises that you purposefully quit Invidia to further your own aims? And he will realise.'

'I know Nagash,' said Mannfred. 'I have known him for a long time.'

'Darling, I was flirting with eternal damnation centuries before you were but a mere pang of thirst in your sire's gullet,' the Mortarch laughed with genuine mirth. Unable to dispute the point, Mannfred simply continued.

'I fought alongside him at Geigohenge. I saw him advance on the walls – alone. I saw those walls crumble into sand at his mere presence. I watched him take cannonballs like they were the bites of a gnat. I saw him raise a graveyard – an entire graveyard – with the twitch of a finger. I watched him reduce the Stormling lord and her heavens-drake to dust with a touch.'

It was that memory that stuck in Mannfred's mind. It wasn't just how the warrior and her mount had screamed; it was the sheer dispassion of it. Nagash had not even looked at the champion as he passed sentence. Mannfred had once believed that, like himself, Nagash simply disregarded concepts such as nobility and honour. Now he wondered if the Great Necromancer even understood them at all in anything but the most abstract fashion.

'I saw all that, and still I committed to my course. So what does that tell you of my resolve?'

The Nulahmian queen was no longer smiling. Neferata's eyes had often been described by her simpering suitors as possessing a hawk-like clarity; Mannfred instead thought of it as a vulture's scavenging gaze, though he recognised that this was simply pettiness speaking. Nevertheless, the vampire suppressed a wave of unease as his fellow Mortarch gave a humourless chuckle.

'Take care, von Carstein. I found Narazar vaguely charming, and you'll see what's left of him soon enough. Imagine what I have planned for you.' With that she was gone, her image dissipating into the slick mirror-pool. Even when he was alone again, Mannfred's voice did not rise above a whisper.

'We'll see.'

MANNFRED VON CARSTEIN

Cunning and vindictive, Mannfred von Carstein is numbered amongst the most dangerous of all Soulblight vampires. An accomplished warrior, sorcerer and general, he has long served as one of Nagash's foremost warlords, though his ambitions extend far beyond such servitude.

Soaring above the battlefield upon the dread abyssal Ashigaroth, Mannfred von Carstein watches the advance of his armies with bitter pride. His pale face curls in a sneer, calculating red eyes assessing every charge and desperate defence for weaknesses. When the prey is sighted, he directs his monstrous mount in a blistering dive; spells and arrows rebound harmlessly from the baroque plates of the Armour of Templehof, while storms of deathly magic rip asunder his adversaries' very souls. The moment he hits the enemy line, Mannfred begins to slaughter. Warriors fall like tumbling Lethisian bone-tiles before his wicked sickle-glaive and Gheistvor, the Sword of Unholy Power. The spirit essence of those slain is captured by the ancient vampire, channelled and redirected through malignant incantations. Those who fall are soon resurrected by Mannfred's dire sorceries and added to the hosts of his shambling minions, a cruel laugh leaving the Soulblight as he watches these risen foes fall upon their former friends.

Mannfred was not the first von Carstein to haunt the World-that-Was, but he was the most infamous. The vampire's conniving ways led in part to Nagash's resurrection, but his spite played a significant role in the destruction of that world. One might have expected Nagash to condemn Mannfred's soul to an eternity of tormenting purgatory for this, but the Great Necromancer is loath to throw away any tool that may prove useful. Thus was Mannfred summoned once more to serve as the Mortarch of Night, commander of a great legion of the dead. Though he despises servitude, even Mannfred – for all his self-absorbed bitterness – knows that he cannot hope to simply overpower Nagash. For now, he plays the role of the loyal servant, fuelled by disgust at his status and commanding the Legion of Night even as he plots to free himself. Nagash is well aware of his Mortarch's untrustworthy nature, but he is willing to overlook his treacherous intentions for now – besides, such constant scheming ensures the vampire's mind remains a sharp and potent weapon to be used against Nagash's enemies.

Outside the ranks of the gods, only Arkhan the Black and perhaps Vokmortian exceed Mannfred's skill at necromancy, a state of affairs that the vampire is constantly striving to alter. With a pulse of will, Mannfred can animate a score of corpses, sending them against his enemies in a relentless tide. He can fashion a cyclone of spectral blades to assail the foe or conjure a gale of spirits that fill the air with soul-shredding shrieks. Yet Mannfred's greatest weapon remains his mind. The Battle of Rotsoul Mire, the War of the Nail, the Invidian Invasion: on all these occasions and more, the Mortarch of Night has shown himself willing to do whatever it takes to ensure victory, no matter how dirty or dishonourable the deed may be. It is a trait that has proven worthwhile time and again. While many vampires may look upon the greatest of the von Carsteins with private disdain, none can deny his ruthless efficiency in the power games they all play – nor shake off their unease that, one day, his black star might rise further still.

NEFERATA

From the opulent city of Nulahmia, Neferata weaves a tapestry of strife and discord that stretches across the Mortal Realms. But she is no mere instigator skulking fearfully in the shadows; she is a queen amongst vampires, and when she takes to the battlefield in person, few can stand before her dark majesty.

Neferata is the first of the Soulblight. Though she may appear youthful, with her skin a flawless alabaster and her hair a lustrous black, in truth, she is many millennia old. She recalls a time when even Nagash was mortal, and it was her brilliance and will to power that led in part to the creation of the vampires. As a member of the ancient cabal that plumbed the Nine Books of Nagash for the secrets of immortality and the first to achieve true undeath, Neferata has claimed to be the ultimate sire of every lesser dynasty and bloodline – though her old rival Mannfred would surely dispute such a notion, much to her amusement. The sheer aura of majesty she projects is a potent weapon in itself, and it is small wonder that Nagash granted Neferata the dark honour of being numbered amongst his inner circle of Mortarchs.

While some may fixate upon Neferata's cold beauty or quicksilver speed, the wise know that her greatest weapon has always been her intelligence. For many centuries, she has honed her craft and her cunning, and now all but the most intricate of stratagems are little more than a game to her. Nulahmia is a hotbed of intrigue and conspiracy, but such is the Blood Queen's mastery of her sinister arts that she can track the progress of a great multitude of expert spies, secretive cults and devoted generals simultaneously, directing them with consummate skill to serve her ends. Only for the most sensitive of manipulations – or to stave off ennui and amuse herself fighting against those rare foes she deems worthy of personal attention – will Neferata quit the luxurious palaces of Nulahmia and ride at the head of her Legion of Blood. Mounted atop the dread abyssal Nagadron, she impassively surveys the enemy army as it draws up before her, its composition, tactics and secret weaknesses having already been revealed by her vast network of informers, and a thousand counter-ploys run through the vampire's mind.

Neferata is as skilled a sorcerer as any vampire, capable of reanimating shattered undead minions with a thought or temporarily rendering her warriors as transient and difficult to strike as dusk's cloying mist. It is in the arena of personal combat, however, where the Soulblight queen excels, for when she does bestride the battlefield, Neferata intends to make a statement. She bears to war relics of ancient blood cults enchanted with agonising magics: Akmet-har, the Dagger of Jet, has opened the throats of countless sacrifices splayed across gore-slick altars, its killing edge constantly hungering for new victims, while Aken-seth, the Staff of Pain, ensures that those touched by her spells are soon overcome with waves of blood-burning torment. Most who encounter the queen are either slain by precise strikes too fast for even an aelf's eye to follow or else left for Nagadron to crush and devour.

Only for the most notable of adversaries, those who display the greatest skill or conviction, does Neferata expend any real effort. With malicious laughter and calculating sneers, she will toy with them, inflicting death by a thousand cuts and sapping their strength little by little. Every weakness will be exploited, if only to impose upon such unfortunates the folly of defying her. As they fall, these champions are granted one final reward for the fleeting entertainment provided: their blood is used to feed Neferata's monstrous hunger, their last sensation that of the vampire queen's sharpened fangs plunging deep into their neck.

'I will not deny that there is a certain crass appeal to be found in lifting a silvered blade aloft to the cheers of one's sycophants or – as my kind are far more wont to do – drowning the lands in a tide of hot blood and revelling in the predictable fear of the unwashed masses. There are even some who would argue that these realms were built through such unsubtle means. But I know better. I alone appreciate the nature of victory, and that is because I alone recognise the enemy. Not the greenskins, not the moronic chanters of the Ruinous Powers, not even the Storm God's mongrel legions. The enemy is chance: the flip of the peddler's coin, the rolling of the gambler's knucklebones. My power is born from mastery, and that mastery is over disaster. I see outcomes like the branches of a great gnarled oak, and I prune away all those that do not please me. I know the way the coin will land, because I ensured that I minted it. I make certain that the knucklebones are weighted before my foes even decide to pick them up. So it is that those who would oppose me soon discover that there is no chance. There is only my will.'

- Queen Neferata, Meditations upon Dominion

LAUKA VAI, MOTHER OF NIGHTMARES

A twisted amalgamation of bat-fiend, drake and vampire, Lauka Vai stands paramount amongst the Vengorian Lords, the most monstrous inheritors of the Soulblight curse. Yet despite her hideous appearance, the Mother of Nightmares holds to a creed of nobility even as she forever battles against her punishing red hunger.

Lauka Vai is that rarest of things – a vampire with a sliver of conscience. Though she appears as a grotesque flesh-meld, what remains of her soul is that of a fierce warrior queen. Once, she was the finest sword of the Askurga Renkai, an order of Ghurish vampire-knights who, though they bore no love for mortals, refused to prey upon those weaker than themselves. When the Age of Chaos came, they fought courageously to defy the Ruinous Powers. A quest towards the Realm's Edge to slay a vile Tzeentchian sorcerer was to rewrite Lauka's fate, however. Long had she trained herself in the art of drawing upon the beast within while never succumbing entirely to its rages. But during the battle with the sorcerer, she was cast into a tar pit oozing with primordial Ghurish magic and emerged with her body warped into that of a nightmare. Upon her return, the proud knights of the Askurga Renkai sought to slay their champion, believing her to be inherently corrupt. In an outraged frenzy, Vai tore them apart with her talons. Horrified at her fratricide, she fled into the dunes.

For years, Lauka fought alone, roaming the desolate wilds and continuing to battle against wild beasts and ruinous warlords. On the occasions that she was witnessed by holdout peoples, she was forced to flee – that is, if she did not succumb to her hunger and fury, committing outrages that gnawed at her tirelessly when the red mist finally abated. But the Necroquake changed Lauka's future a second time. The monstrous Vengorians who ruled the Avengorii Dynasty took great pains to seek out the Mother of Nightmares, for they had heard of her exploits and considered her a paragon of their twisted ilk. Though the embracing of one's own savagery offended Lauka's warrior creed, she also could not deny that it was the first true companionship she had known for some time. Coarse the Avengorii may have been, but they deserved a champion who would deliver them worthy war.

Now Lauka Vai rules as a queen amongst monsters, leading her bestial hosts against the hordes of Chaos and Destruction, whom she considers the finest adversaries. Like all Vengorians, she is thoroughly suffused with ending-magics capable of corroding a blade in seconds or summoning gory downpours of black blood, yet Lauka's greatest weapon is her ironclad will. Even the corpse-monsters favoured by the Avengorii are infused with the Mother of Nightmares' sheer force of personality, battling with unmatched focus in her shadow. But there is a cost. Should Lauka's self-control slip in the heat of the moment, the violence she is capable of is terrible to behold. Each time, she finds it more difficult to pull back from the brink of insanity. If her mind were ever to break entirely, the fate of Ghur's living denizens would be bloody indeed.

VENGORIAN LORDS

If one wishes to gaze upon the monstrous nature that lurks within every Soulblight vampire, they need look no further than the Vengorian Lords. Misshapen and twisted, these hybrid creatures are wracked with self-loathing and vent it upon any foolish enough to gaze upon their repugnant forms. What they cannot bring themselves to admit is that almost all chose their fate, condemned by their own lust for power. Those vampires who were to become Vengorians were most attuned to magic. They detected the first stirrings of Nagash's great spell of demise and travelled to cities close to Nagashizzar to bathe in the coming amethyst storm nearest to the source. When the Necroquake broke, they received far more than they bargained for. Even these lords of evil could not endure such potent ending-magics and remain unchanged. From the waist down, their bodies became twisted amalgamations of chiropteran behemoth and loathsome reptile, a thing of mismatched limbs, tattered wings and rending claws. Though they told themselves that they had mastered the Necroquake, in truth, they were abominations, and they retreated into the most inimical places to brood upon their own faded glory. Vengorian Lords emerge from their lairs only to lead crusades of spiteful retribution, a manifestation of their self-hate. While some claim to be the truest and most beautiful of vampires, privately all but the most demented recognise that they are little better than the wretched abhorrants or other degenerate beasts of the grave. To deny the truth of what has become of them, a Vengorian will order their minions to smash mirrors in advance of their arrival, construct elaborate ballroom masks and monstrous, form-fitting gowns from the stitched-together flesh of the dead, and even sorcerously compel an enemy's wargear to rust, stripping it of its reflective sheen. Even a goblet of fresh vitae might lead such a beast to catch sight of their dreadful appearance, and so Vengorians feed near exclusively upon scabbed and clotted blood. They can harness death magic to conjure bleak squalls that belch forth showers of festering gore or even transmute entire freshwater lakes into turgid, bloody ooze. A land claimed by a Vengorian Lord will inevitably succumb to desiccation and drought, but if this prevents these selfish creatures from having to gaze upon the ruin of their ambition, they consider it a fair trade.

CHAMPIONS OF THE GRAVE

At the head of the Gravelord armies stride immortal champions, pale of flesh and wicked of eye. Whether bolstering their hordes through the arcane power of necromancy or tearing through the terrified living with sickening ease, these vampires are some of Nagash's deadliest warriors.

VAMPIRE LORDS

Vampire Lords are amongst the most terrifying of all undead. Each possesses the strength of several men, reactions to match even a Hyshian blademaster, instinctive command of the black arts and a cunning as sharp as it is cruel. Their powers are multifarious and sinister: many can boil a foe's blood within their veins with but a single arcane phrase or transform into clouds of sanguine-tinted mist to cross the battlefield swiftly.

Vampires are wellsprings of Shyishan magic, and such is their force of will that their very presence bolsters the hordes they raise to prosecute their wars. As they endure the long centuries, a vampire only grows more dangerous; lifetimes of warfare sharpen their skills to levels far beyond that of mortalkind, and their command of necromancy deepens. These elder creatures are known as Vampire Lords, and all would do well to fear them. They are capable of battering aside a mortal shieldwall on their own, and so contemptuous of life are they that even in the midst of battle, a Vampire Lord will sink their fangs into the neck of a worthy adversary, draining their vitae in deep gulps. Some even carry profane chalices filled with the blood of butchered holy men from which they sup and empower themselves when the need arises.

Though many vampires while away their existence in debauched luxury, when war calls, they don a fearsome aspect: accompanied by flights of shrieking bats, they clad themselves in bladed armour emblazoned with dynastic sigils. Some Vampire Lords, particularly the half-bestial chieftains that rule the blood-clans of Ghur, fight at the forefront of every engagement, whilst others focus on strengthening their warriors through necromancy.

A rare few – inevitably the most martially inclined – take to battle atop the majestic form of an arisen Zombie Dragon. Not only does this grant them a hulking mount that can annihilate swathes of enemies with contemptuous ease, it also provides a glorious vantage point from which to see and be seen upon the battlefield – Vampire Lords are proud creatures, and little stirs their lifeless hearts more than filling a foe's last moments with a sense of utter powerlessness and soul-draining terror.

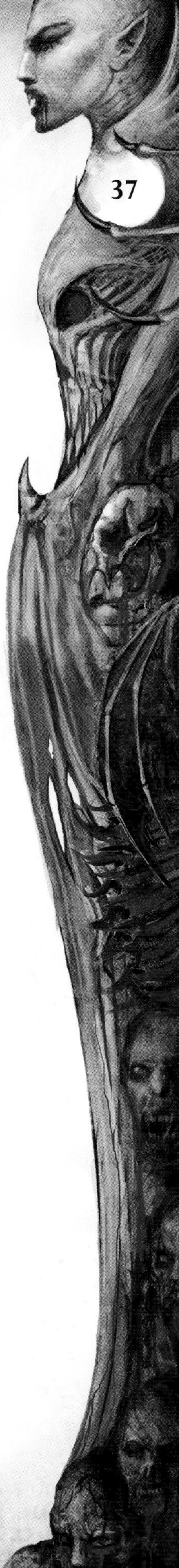

PRINCE VHORDRAI

Prince Vhordrai is widely considered to be the first amongst vampire knights in skill if not in lineage; wild rumour abounds that he has fought and defeated warriors from every species and creed ever to have walked the realms. Mounted atop the great undead drake Shordemaire and wielding the gore-drinking Bloodlance, he leads the hosts of the Kastelai Dynasty out from their ever-shifting fastness, the Crimson Keep, to bring swift death to the foes of the Great Necromancer. Many vampiric warriors venerate him as the purest example of their kind and eagerly pursue the Crimson Keep so that they may ride at his side.

Yet Vhordrai is as much a prisoner as a conqueror. In the aftermath of the Battle of Black Skies, he sought to end Nagash's tyranny for all time, intending to hurl the Great Necromancer's remains through the corrupted realmgate of Yulghuan so that they might be devoured by the Dark Gods. It was a brash plan, and one that Arkhan the Black went to great lengths to oppose. In a clash of sorcery and steel, Vhordrai was narrowly defeated by the First Mortarch and sealed within a realmstone coffin for an age. Only when Nagash returned was the now half-insane Vhordrai released and mystically bound to the Crimson Keep, doomed to an agonising demise should he vacate its walls for more than a day. To so tightly leash such an ambitious creature satisfied the Undying King's twisted sense of justice, and so Vhordrai became the Fist of Nagash, delighting in the ruination of his master's foes even as he raged at his bondage.

Now, however, Nagash's physical form has been shattered once more, and Vhordrai wonders if he has been offered a second chance at freedom. It would be no mean feat to cast off his binding curse, let alone see Nagash destroyed once and for all. Still, the lord of the Kastelai has learnt the value of patience over the long centuries, and he would not risk defying the Great Necromancer twice without good cause.

BLOOD KNIGHTS

Blood Knights are elite vampiric warriors who have dedicated their long existence to mastering the arts of combat. Mounted atop hulking undead chargers known as Nightmares and clad in thick suits of scalloped plate, they ride at the forefront of the Gravelord hosts. Though vampires of a more circumspect persuasion may believe the Blood Knights to be arrogant or reckless, in reality, these cavaliers are simply practised at employing their deadly skills and the unique boons of unlife to the fullest. A Blood Knight can direct their Nightmare with pinpoint precision; as their steeds are immune to pain and distraction, they compel them to trample ranks of lesser warriors without slowing as they search for worthy foes. Blood Knights revel in the spray of arterial gore across their armour as they open throats and veins, invigorated by the carnage and eternally compelled to pursue new heights of battlefield glory.

Blood Knights often assemble into household guards and roving warrior orders, each with their own traditions. It is said that their primogenitor cured his thirst by drinking the blood of a king amongst dragons, and many Blood Knights choose to bear the image of a snarling drake upon their banners in recognition of this feat. The Order of the Bloody Rose seeks out battle far and wide, even allying with the living should it provide greater opportunities for slaughter. The Brethren of the Wolf Rampant ride alongside the hosts of Radukar, laughing as they hunt those who seek to flee Ulfenkarn. But though Blood Knights may adhere to strict martial codes, and some even possess a perverse sense of honour and a desire to master their inherent bloodthirst, at their core, many are murderous beasts obsessed with glory, combat and hearing the screams of the dying beneath their steeds' ironshod hooves.

VARGHEISTS

Vargheists are malformed horrors, winged and monstrous in appearance. Though they were once proud Soulblight nobles, their sanity has been utterly eroded by the need to rend the flesh of the living. With sharpened talons and rows of needle-like fangs, they eviscerate all in their path, desperate to sup upon hot gore. When their frenzied feast is concluded, the Vargheists will take to the sky once more, following the muscled abominations known as Vargoyles in search of fresh prey-things. These, inevitably, will be the first living beings they encounter, for Vargheists care only for indulging their thirsts. More civilised vampires look upon Vargheists with disdain, but this repugnance is coloured with an undercurrent of fear – beneath their projected air of finery, they have far more in common with the monstrous Vargheists then they would ever wish to admit.

Blood starvation is a common punishment amongst the Soulblight dynasties; many patriarchs and matriarchs employ it as a means of torturing rivals or disciplining offspring, while some Blood Knights test themselves by willingly denying their thirst for as long as possible. Should a vampire be deprived of blood for too long, the beast within may overwhelm them and see them permanently devolve into a maddened Vargheist. For some vampires, however, this transformation is seen as embracing their truest nature. Most famous are the Avengorii, whose *mas'ranga* ritual has been adopted by many other Ghurish lineages. The Legion of Blood also possesses a great number of Vargheists; Neferata finds cold amusement in watching vampiric suitors destroy themselves in pursuit of her favour and relishes commanding the beasts to make a gory display of any who earn her ire.

AN UNDYING MAJESTY

The proudest vampires take to battle upon thrones forged through necromantic artifice, swarms of bloated bats shrieking around them. Yet only a fool would believe these undead languid or slothful – they can erupt into quicksilver motion in an instant, empowering themselves with freshly imbibed gore.

COVEN THRONES

Gliding through the night with an ominous grace, Coven Thrones are carriages of fused sinew and bone held aloft by processions of tormented souls. Upon rich satin cushions, a Vampire Lady and her favoured handmaidens recline, gazing upon vistas of bloodshed with an air of cold disinterest. Vampires are often haughty creatures, befitting their status as the progeny of Nagash, and only those most consumed with the thrill of the hunt trek through the filth of a battlefield by choice. Others seek more refined means of closing with their prey, and it was from such a desire that the first Coven Thrones were created. Suitably ensconced, a Vampire Lady is saved the indignity of walking or slaughtering lesser beings and is instead given licence to pursue those adversaries she deems worthy of personal attention.

Many vampires are strangely beguiling, and the Vampire Lady is capable of entrancing a soul with but a glance. When this transfixing aura is focused, even the most stalwart of heroes can be rendered putty in her hands. The most intriguing are granted the blood kiss and are destined to serve as their mistress's champions and paramours until her amusement with them expires. Most, however, are simply bled dry with razor-sharp stilettos and poniards, pulled close and devoured by the hungering undead maidens.

Yet Coven Thrones are not simply bleakly regal conveyances, and those who ride upon them are not merely indolent gluttons. A Vampire Lady will choose her handmaidens not only for their beauty but also for their skills as augurs and haruspices; the blood of those unfortunates they slay is collected and pooled in a enchanted bowl mounted upon their carriage, from which the vampires can glean visions of potential futures. So forewarned, a Vampire Lady can direct her minions with a prescient precision upon the battlefield as well as ward herself against the predictable blows of those few souls capable of resisting her bewitching charms.

BLOODSEEKER PALANQUINS

All vampires constantly feel the urge to drink the blood of the living, but for those known as Sanguinarchs, this imperative has become an all-consuming obsession. Creatures fitting their description feature in hushed folklore throughout the realms: Bloodmothers, Red Spiders and Pale Doyennes, to name but a few. Sanguinarchs are devoted to the pursuit of the perfect vintage. They are one of the most common breeds of vampire to secretly embed themselves within mortal societies,

THE SOULBLIGHT CURSE

It has been remarked that superstitions are drawn to Shyish as readily as souls. Vampires have stalked the Amethyst Realm since time immemorial, and so plenty of this grim folklore revolves around these most sinister undead. With that said, there is a notable lack of concrete information concerning the weaknesses of these creatures; much of this hard-won knowledge is hoarded by vampire-hunting conclaves such as the Silver Circlet and the Hawthorns, and even these are not immune to being misled by canny undead wishing to protect their secrets.

What is known is that vampires are almost exclusively human in origin. Some say that this is because of a jealous curse inflicted by Elder Bones, though it is just as likely that vampires simply prefer to grant the blood kiss to those of a similar origin or that the longer-lived races have less inclination to seek immortality. Even so, the legends of Necros claim that at least one aelf has succumbed to the curse over the millennia.

Beyond this, tales vary wildly, with each underworld, kingdom and even hamlet possessing its own lore concerning vampires. Much of this, unfortunately for the inhabitants, is entirely apocryphal. Vampires are not destroyed by Hysh's light, though most loathe its scouring brilliance and take refuge beneath palls of darkness and colossal swarms of bats where possible. They do not need permission to enter a royal abode and are not halted by scattered sourwart seeds or flowing rivers, though some vampires of lesser power and will can be warded away by fastening an upside-down straw doll to the door with a silver nail or covering oneself in week-old ashsprig. The only sure way to end the evil of a vampire, however, is to utterly destroy its physical form, for should even a sliver remain intact, the unhallowed creature may reform over time. Such is easier said than done, for vampires are ferocious foes, and even when they retreat to their lairs to slumber, their undead guardians never sleep, never tire and are merciless in the destruction of intruders.

for such provides greater access to intriguing flavours; playing the part of reclusive socialites or eccentric aristocrats, they quietly manipulate bonds of aristocratic marriage and noble liaisons, refining a bloodline over centuries until it has become a truly indulgent concoction. The Legion of Blood counts many Sanguinarchs as its finest agents, for Nulahmian vampires are often infused with a lust for the finer things in unlife. Some Sanguinarchs, however, believe that only battle can spice blood to its utmost piquancy. It is these thirsting horrors who are most commonly found amongst Gravelord armies, offering their martial skills in exchange for a chance to further their haemovorous quest.

Surrounded by flights of spiteful banshees whose wails can freeze a mortal heart, Bloodseeker Palanquins make for an unnerving sight as they drift across the battlefield, their owner languorously draped across fine cushions. These vampires are masters of exsanguinatory magics, capable of compelling a foe's blood to vacate their body in an explosive spray from their eyes, nose and mouth. In truth, battle itself presents little interest to the Sanguinarchs; rather, it is blood alone that holds their attention. No vampire can resist the urge to salivate as they watch such a creature at work, blending stolen vitae into draughts of unparalleled sweetness and potency. Soulblight creatures who sup upon such artisan blood-broths are filled with an unnatural vigour, assailing their foes with redoubled fervour as the Sanguinarch lets out a cruel, lilting laugh.

FELL BATS

Swooping low through the midnight skies, Fell Bats pursue their prey with a single-minded ferocity. Each of these bloated carrion-beasts is crafted through dark magics and a diet of tainted blood, and they are swollen far beyond their lesser chiropteran brethren. A fully grown Fell Bat's wingspan can outsize even a Chaos Warrior, and their wiry frames are strong enough to pluck a fully armoured knight from the saddle of a charging Demigryph and carry them away into the darkening skies. Their fangs are sharp and deadly, and a Fell Bat that has sampled the taste of blood will swiftly fly into an eviscerating frenzy, only ceasing its attack once it – or, more likely, its prey – has been gorily torn asunder.

Fell Bats do not hunt through sight or sound; rather, they can sense those mortals with the most vital blood gushing through their veins. They are a common sight throughout Shyish; in settlements throughout the Prime Innerlands, superstition abounds that one can tell one's fortune by counting the number of Fell Bats circling the crooked tops of cathedral spires. What few realise is that Fell Bats are more than simple predators. Many are enchanted, serving as the literal eyes of their masters, and they fulfil a sinister purpose. The blood they drink is not consumed wholesale but held as a liquid mass within the Fell Bat's throat. Once 'full', they will return to their creator's lair in their multitudes to hang upside-down in darkened caves and undercrofts. Masked thralls will slowly march between the rows of Fell Bats, carefully opening their throats and draining the blood into bowls to serve to their master. So do the leather-winged beasts allow the vampires to indulge their thirsts without quitting their strongholds and ensure that terror of the undead spreads far and wide.

THE BLOOD OF THE WOLF

The Vyrkos are a strange and savage clan of vampires; possessed of an animalistic curse, they delight in the hunt even more than their kin. Whether dwelling within the dark forests of Shyish or ruling the cursed city of Ulfenkarn, the lords of the dynasty are predators beyond compare.

RADUKAR

Radukar the Wolf is the most infamous of all Vyrkos. One of those rare mortals who actively sought transformation into a vampire, an aging Radukar tracked the shamanistic elders of the dynasty, proving his worth by slaying the twin-headed wolf Vilnas with his bare hands and reclaiming the barrow-blade of the infamous vampiric emperor Morkan. Upon being granted the blood kiss, Radukar's will proved sufficient to control the animalistic rage that howled within his mind; his triple-masted carrack, the *Impaler's Gift*, soon became a feared sight along the coasts of Shyish. Though he possesses a rugged, dark charisma, Radukar is a predator at heart. He revels in the headlong charge at pursuit's end, for in these moments, he can unshackle the bestial rage within him and let loose an ear-splitting howl that infuses his minions with a measure of his own fury.

'In life, I would have cut down all of you in the span of a single breath and picked my teeth clean with your bones. Can you imagine what I will do to you now?'

- Radukar the Wolf

Since his ousting from the Ebon Citadel of Ulfenkarn, a monstrous transformation has overcome Radukar. Now he towers above even his vampiric kin. His body bristles with coarse hair, while his nails have extended into sharpened talons. With a single blow, he can punch through armour, flesh and bone to grasp a beating heart and rip it out, and his furious howls draw packs of Dire Wolves to the hunt from miles around. Yet though he has become a beast in body as well as soul, there may still be more to Radukar than meets the eye, as his living prey will no doubt discover to their cost.

THE COURT OF THE WOLF

During his rulership of Ulfenkarn, Radukar bound a great many minions and allies to his cause, the greatest of whom are all notable foes in their own right. At the head of his Thirsting Court stands Torgillius, a venerable Deathmage from the arcane sepulchrist order known as the Pact Mortalis. He claims to have unlocked the secrets of the grave-sand phylacteries used by the lords of Ulfenkarn, and the scurrying undead vermin that infest the city are said to be his eyes and ears. Gorslav is a mysterious masked being of unknown provenance who shambles through the sprawling graveyards and calls up fresh hordes of Deadwalkers to overwhelm invaders. In life, Watch Captain Halgrim betrayed his fellows to Radukar in exchange for immortality as a vampire, but instead of receiving the blood kiss, he was slain and raised as a skeletal automaton to command the Deathrattle of the Ulfenwatch in accordance with the Wolf's wishes.

Radukar is often accompanied by members of the Kosargi Nightguard; these revenant ogors serve as loyally in death as they did in life, their imposing bulk more than sufficient to dissuade any who would seek to slay the Wolf. Through the shadows prowl vampiric offspring known as the Vyrkos Blood-born, cruel and swift hunters forever on the verge of being overwhelmed by their curse. Yet perhaps most fearsome of all are the Vargskyr, the remnants of those Vyrkos who could not control their animalistic nature. Their minds shattered and flesh transmuted until they became colossal bat-like beasts, these horrors patiently stalk their prey before ripping them asunder in displays of staggering violence.

BELLADAMMA VOLGA

Belladamma Volga is the first of the Vyrkos. Little is known of this wizened matriarch beyond the strange legends of the Prime Innerlands. In Stygxx, it is said that to see her once upon the horizon, silhouetted by Lunaghast's sinister glow, is an omen of impending disaster; twice heralds the death of a lover; and should a mortal see her three times, only the gods can save them from her pursuit. In Dhûmi, there is a tale of a starving girl-child lost in the woods who encountered Volga and was given a bowl of steaming broth. Twice she asked the vampire to help her hungering family, and twice she was denied. Upon the third request, Volga magically transmuted the girl's kin into slavering wolves, laughing as they feasted upon the rest of their village.

Belladamma rides to battle mounted atop the hulking wolf Rothabak, who some say was once one of the matriarch's ill-fated suitors. At her side lope lupine companions and packs of slavering Dire Wolves, all of whom are subservient to their fierce she-alpha. Though a skilled swordswoman, Volga's true talents lie in the arts of sorcery. No Vyrkos has as intuitive a command over their savage curse as she. With but a gesture, she can see a foe wracked by terrible transfigurations, their body contorting and face elongating into a muzzle as cries of terror turn to bloodthirsty howls. Soon, one more wolf prowls alongside Volga's nomadic pack, hunting her foes with mindless obedience and battling for scraps left behind from the vampire's bloody feasts.

LADY ANNIKA, THE THIRSTING BLADE

One of the undead nobles battling for control of Ulfenkarn, the wraith-thin creature known as Lady Annika is a Vyrkos unlike any other. Not for her the fury and cunning of the wolf; instead, her curse manifests as the endless thirst of the blood-sucking bat. Though she may wander the Ebon Citadel bemoaning the endless passage of years and scarcity of decent dressmakers to be found, this is but a mask that Annika adopts in an attempt to hide her true, vile nature. In reality, her chambers are filled with corpses that have been messily exsanguinated and dismembered, all to feed the vampire's voracious metabolism.

Annika's thirst for blood is profound – a grim irony, for as Ulfenkarn's mistress of ceremonies, she was renowned for her precise appetite – and the cramps of starvation set in almost as soon as she satiates them. Such explains her maniacal focus on slaying foes as swiftly as possible to gorge upon their precious ichor; it is even gossiped by her fellow Vyrkos that she ingests vials of blood tinged with the quicksilver realmstone known as chamonite, heightening her reflexes without heed of any transmuting side-effects. From her lair in the Screaming Spires, a cluster of grim towers built upon the flanks of the Ebon Citadel, Annika orders her minions to abduct Ulfenkarn's people on a mass scale to feed her hungers.

Armed with the Blade Proboscian, an enchanted rapier capable of draining a foe of blood with but a scratch, Annika plunges into the thickest melees without pause. Here the image of the elegant aristocrat falls away entirely, replaced with a shrieking monster that cares for nothing save the spray of hot vitae across its lips.

KRITZA, THE RAT PRINCE

Once a noble of Ulfenkarn, the vain Kritza sought to undermine the Wolf, professing outward loyalty while playing the double agent. Far from being an altruistic yearning, his efforts were born of a selfish desire to ingratiate himself with any potential liberators of Ulfenkarn. Radukar, however, was not deceived. Savaged to within an inch of obliteration by the Wolf, Kritza was forced to flee.

Hiding in a Corpse Cart, and having unknowingly been granted the blood kiss, Kritza drank the brackish blood of vermin to sustain himself. By the time his body was dumped into a plague pit, his curse had manifested in the aspect of the rodents he had gorged upon. Kritza fled into the sewers, husbanding his powers and developing a kinship with the rats of the subterranean Teeming Warrens. Only when Radukar was deposed did he emerge to stake a claim to rulership, accompanied by his 'vermintide' – a vast swarm of rodents both living and dead.

Now Kritza plays the part of the noble once more, covering his heinous sewer-stench with nauseous Nulahmian perfumes. Should Kritza be sufficiently wounded, he will transform into a tide of shrieking rats, scurrying away before reforming again. More than one foe has thought the Rat Prince slain only to be suddenly impaled from behind by Kritza's blade, the vampire disdainfully striding over their corpse with a superior sneer.

THE DEATHRATTLE LEGIONS

Marching in relentless unity, their fleshless hands clutching rusted weapons, the Deathrattle legions advance with grim and unstoppable purpose. These skeletal hosts are the remnants of bygone ages risen through the power of necromancy and chained to the will of their undying monarchs.

WIGHT KINGS

In life, the Wight Kings were conquerors, warlords and absolute monarchs whose domains stretched across swathes of the realms. Since relinquishing their grip on mortality, little has changed. Clad in verdigrised armour and tattered finery, these skeletal rulers now hold dominion over the Deathrattle Kingdoms – entire nations of the living dead. Death, however, has not blunted their hunger for conquest and war, and so they march to battle at the head of vast skeletal armies. Those living souls whose lands are invaded by a Deathrattle legion are destined either to be subjugated and enslaved by their new revenant master or else dispassionately slaughtered and used to reinforce the ranks of the Wight King's armies.

Though a Wight King's morality may have been deadened in the centuries since their death, the tactical acumen that once fed their conquests remains as sharp as ever. Unburdened by concepts such as doubt and weariness, the Deathrattle phalanxes react instantly to their lord's commands, prosecuting his will with a relentless and morbid determination. While some Wight Kings – particularly those who ruled over hot-blooded nations in Aqshy and Ghur – relish the chance to cover their bones in fresh gore, many hold back until a final push is needed to turn an enemy's wavering into a true rout. Only then do they stride forth at the head of their household guard or lead the charge of mounted barrow-knights. Though their armour may be rusted and patinated, the Shyishan sorceries that cling to them allow the Wight Kings to withstand even the most punishing blows. Their armouries are stocked with ancient blades and lances bearing dire, vorpal curses capable of snatching away a living soul or freezing a warrior's heart with the merest of scratches.

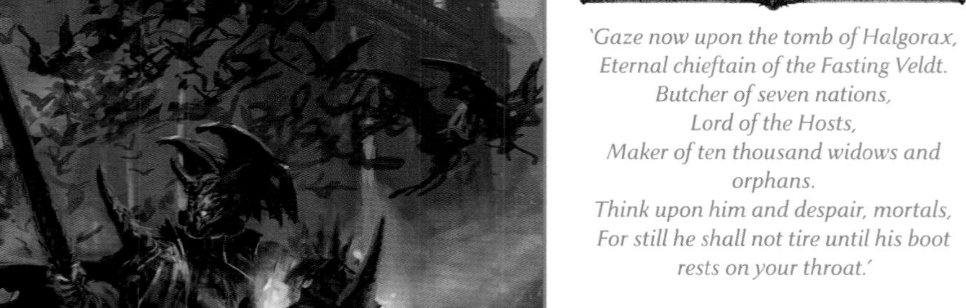

'Gaze now upon the tomb of Halgorax,
Eternal chieftain of the Fasting Veldt.
Butcher of seven nations,
Lord of the Hosts,
Maker of ten thousand widows and orphans.
Think upon him and despair, mortals,
For still he shall not tire until his boot rests on your throat.'

- Inscription above the entrance to the Hollow Barrows of Ghur

Whether they were once a cruel Shyishan despot or an enlightened Hyshian philosarch, all Wight Kings retain a sense of pride and individuality – now that the pleasures of life are but a fading memory, this is all that remains to them. Such is their imperious will that it is difficult for any save Nagash and his Mortarchs to bind them into service, as many lesser vampires and Deathmages have discovered to their cost. Wise Soulblight monarchs instead form alliances and binding pacts with the Wight Kings, offering them the freedom of conquest and mountains of corpses with which to reinforce their hosts. In turn, the vampires gain the allegiance of singularly effective battlefield champions and lieutenants. While some Wight Kings, most infamously the Jade Skull Emperor who holds dominion over Shyish's Warmsoul Uplands, cling to their independence, most are willing to heed such terms. With the rise of the Ossiarch Bonereapers and the avaricious eyes these construct warriors turn upon the Deathrattle Kingdoms, many Wight Kings have come to appreciate the value of powerful allies.

GRAVE GUARD

The elite champions and housecarls of the Deathrattle Kingdoms, bands of Grave Guard can be found wherever the Wight Kings stride. In life, each of these skeletal praetorians numbered amongst not only the most deadly warriors in service to their lords but also the most trusted. Many lay down their lives in service to their nation's rulers or swore oaths of eternal service – pacts that, in Shyish and those lands that have felt its chill influence, were taken most literally. Great sepulchres and spell-warded barrows were constructed to house the remains of these honourbound warriors; when their kings and emperors were resurrected as undead wights, so too were the Grave Guard. Still they serve to protect their lieges and carry out their will, and it is often the Grave Guard who form the immovable anchor of a Deathrattle battleline, their ruthless skill honed over centuries of bitter warfare.

In life, the Grave Guard were often shown great favour by their lords, who afforded them the richest pleasures and most noble status as a reward for their service. In death, such favour manifests in their superior wargear: the weapons and armour of the Grave Guard are festooned with fell enchantments and glow with an eerie light. Each cursed blade is capable of passing through even rune-forged Chaos armour with shocking ease, tearing away the soul of the wearer and blasting it into the underworlds of Shyish. Grave Guard often retain more individuality than most Deathrattle, but only enough to carry out their duties and indulge their monarch's desire to reminisce about the days they walked as mortals. When left to their own devices, they will instead keep watch from the alcoves of their mausoleums and barrows, striking down intruders with clinical efficiency. Such is the quality of the Grave Guard as seneschals that many vampires also choose to raise such warriors into service, and the walls of their sinister keeps are eternally patrolled by bands of these remorseless custodians.

BLACK KNIGHTS

The ground thunders and shakes beneath the charge of the Black Knights. These undead cavaliers form the shock regiments of the Deathrattle Kingdoms; mounted atop tireless skeletal steeds, they crash into the foe with the terminal inevitability of death itself. Sheer momentum and the bone-splintering force of their impact buckle shieldwalls in moments, while long heirloom lances skewer flesh and punch through steel plate. Those adversaries who attempt to flee are swiftly rode down by the Black Knights, who perform such culling duties with the same cold satisfaction a rat-catcher would exterminate a nest of scurrying vermin.

Black Knights were once landed nobles and feudal scions, for in those ancient kingdoms, only they had the wealth necessary to maintain a suitable war-steed. Theirs was the honour of riding at the head of their liege's armies, and many Wight Kings still grant their Black Knights the right to launch the first charge of battle – a privilege that often rankles with allied bands of Blood Knights. Black Knights often retain a lingering sense of pride in their status, refusing to dip their lances before one who has not yet earned their respect through conquest. In truth, however, the Black Knights are bound to a single, eternal duty like most Deathrattle, and the satisfaction they find in the fury of the charge is forever fleeting.

DEATHRATTLE SKELETONS

Deathrattle Skeletons form the core of many Soulblight hosts, for there are countless corpses buried beneath the crust of the realms waiting to be raised once more. Clutching corroded weapons and mustering beneath faded banners, they advance in a tireless lockstep – a host of clattering bone marching with terrifying purpose. Though skeletons are not the most fearsome of warriors individually, their utter lack of mercy sees them swarm over the foe in a vast tide, stabbing and hacking without thought for their own protection. The terror engendered by witnessing rank after rank of grinning skeletons at war is a weapon in itself, for only the most courageous can hold their nerve when confronted with such a stark manifestation of their own mortality.

Skeletons are not solely warriors but also the civilians and labourers of the Deathrattle Kingdoms –mindless subjects over whom the dread Wight Kings rule. Without need for rest or sustenance, they will work endlessly in unsettling silence; skeletons can be found mining mountains and stripping forests of wood, tilling pale corn-fields that when shucked leave only fingerbones, and constructing sprawling mausoleums and tomb-complexes to honour their masters. In this way do they contribute to Nagash's necrotopia, raising fiefdoms where sterility and unchanging order hold sway. No realm is safe from this bleak colonisation; in Ghyran, Deathrattle Skeletons infested with corpse-fungi and writhing throttle-vines march through the twisted forests of Decrepita, while in Ghur, their remains are spliced with the bones of that realm's manifold predators, for the vampiric chieftains and corpse-shamans of the plains believe that such will infuse the Deathrattle with the animal fury of these beasts in battle.

MACABRE HORDES

At the heart of many Gravelord armies are the Deadwalkers, fresh corpses that stagger forward as a mindless horde to overwhelm the living. The duty of maintaining their numbers falls to the Deathmages, black-hearted mortals who have descended so deeply into the study of necromancy that it has permeated their very souls.

DEADWALKER ZOMBIES

Deadwalker Zombies are the corpses of the recently dead given animus by the power of necromancy. Rotting flesh clings to their bones, giving off a charnel stink, while decaying vocal cords retain the ability to moan wordlessly. Draped in tattered clothing, some maintain slack grips on crude improvised weapons, though many are content to tear at the living with filth-encrusted nails and teeth. Deadwalkers are utterly mindless, and since the eruption of the Necroquake, migrations of these unliving shamblers have become a common threat to which the denizens of the realms have had to adapt. Bogs, fens and plague pits are all spots from which a Deadwalker march can begin, and many free cities have instituted volunteer bands known as 'pyre-gangs' whose duty is to track and immolate Deadwalker epidemics before they can spread.

Though Deadwalker Zombies are clumsy and slow, their motions impeded by fraying muscles, they should never be underestimated. Even the most honourable of vampires sees these vile beings as chattel to be expended at will; zombies will batter against a fortress wall until either it breaks or they do, and they will march over scorching fields of flame and into storms of arrow fire without pause. Like a cloying quagmire given motion and agency, they drag down the living, many of whom are forced to confront the rotting bodies of their own kin amongst the horde. Worst of all, those slain are liable to be reanimated by the necrotic magic that clings to the Deadwalkers, groaning inanely as they lurch to their feet and stagger murderously towards their allies of moments prior.

DIRE WOLVES

Dire Wolves are the mangy cadavers of the lupine pack hunters that haunt the realms' black forests and bleak tundras. Their predatory instincts have not diminished since their demise; if anything, their hunger to rend and tear living flesh appears only to have increased. Unlike most undead, Dire Wolves are ferociously swift, and the unflagging stamina conferred by their resurrection makes them excellent hunters. Their powerful sense of smell is preserved, and widespread folklore maintains that they are able to sense fear carried upon the winds. The charge of a pack of red-eyed Dire Wolves emerging from the blackness of night is a terrifying thing to behold, for their jaws can crunch through bone with sickening ease and the echoing howls loosed by their alphas fill the mind with the oldest and most primal fears of mortalkind, immobilising the foe in the critical moments before the Dire Wolves pounce.

Many vampires, particularly those who cling to airs of aristocracy, possess a particular fondness for Dire Wolves. They are treated as beloved hunting hounds, and favoured thrall Necromancers are charged with the duty of infusing them with necromantic vigour during battle. No lineage exemplifies this favour more than the Vyrkos, for whom the wolf is a totemic beast of singular importance. Belladamma Volga, the semi-mythical matriarch of the dynasty, is said to sometimes enter battle accompanied only by the elders of her bloodline and vast packs of howling Dire Wolves; entire townships have been overrun by their slavering charges and proud enemy hosts reduced to the status of fleeing, terrified game-beasts.

NECROMANCERS

Surrounded by coiling wisps of Shyishan energies and clutching crooked skull-topped staffs, Necromancers shuffle forwards alongside the shambling hordes of the undead. Though they may appear destitute, clad as they are in filthy rags, their faces hollow and gaunt, these corrupt souls are vital components of the Gravelord armies. At their muttered commands, ranks of the living dead emerge from shallow corpse pits, eyes blazing with amethyst light. Through their forbidden arts are ranks of skeletons and milling mobs of Deadwalkers granted an unholy impetus or the foe overcome with crippling despair.

Though Necromancers are not inherently more gifted than the sepulchrist orders of Shyish or the Amethyst Battlemages of the Collegiate Arcane, they are willing to perform truly horrifying acts in pursuit of power: corpse-snatching and sacrifice, experimentation on the living, unhallowed flesh-melding. Many have been hollowed out by the dark energies they wield. For each foe lanced with a spear of necrotic magic and every arrow thwarted by a hastily raised shield of bone, the Necromancer barters away a little more of their humanity, further chaining them to Nagash's tyrannical will.

It is not difficult to grasp why a mortal might become enthralled by the study of necromancy. Be it the chance to restore life to beloved kin, dreams of raising the dead to take vengeance against a hated rival, or simply the desire to master that most intrinsic of mortal fears: the passage of a soul to the underworlds, every Necromancer has their own tale of why they took the first step on the path. Ultimately, however, all lead to the same destination. With each terrible act they perform, a Necromancer is further numbed to their own corruption, fundamentally divested from the living and, ironically, closer to the deathless state they once sought dominion over. Many Necromancers dream of attaining immortality and becoming feared liche-lords who rule over empires of the grave. Few ever achieve this end; far more common is it for Necromancers to be bound into the service of the Soulblight vampires, the latter sharing a measure of their arcane knowledge with these fawning creatures in return for keeping their cadaverous armies at fighting strength.

CORPSE CARTS

Across those lands in thrall to the Gravelords, mortals have come to fear the creak and rattle of a Corpse Cart approaching through the gloom. These rickety, mouldering wagons are mobile altars of undeath; filled with writhing and moaning cadavers and pulled by shambling Deadwalkers impaled on rusted spikes, they are a ghoulish parody of the plague carts that pass through settlements in times of disease. Each Corpse Cart is driven to battle by a cackling Corpsemaster, withered creatures who are neither mindless zombies nor true Deathmages. They direct their rotting wagons to points where the undead advance falters, the morbid energies surrounding the constructs reknitting bone and deadened flesh to send the shambling hordes rising to their feet once more.

Many Corpse Carts are crowned by profane relics known as unholy lodestones, black-iron tocsins that clang out an endless dirge and draw the magics of undeath to themselves in even greater proportions. Others host blazing braziers on which corrupted realmstone is burnt. The palls of smoke emitted by these flames drift across the battlefield with what seems to be a malignant sentience; arcane energy withers in their wake, while the minds of enemy wizards are wracked with agony so intense that it can induce a temporary insanity.

MORTIS ENGINES

Those few Necromancers who achieve their aim of becoming true masters of undeath are treated with almost reverent awe by their fellows. On the vanishingly rare occasion that such a being is destroyed, their remains are collected up with a fastidious patience by their acolytes, for they still resonate with forbidden power. The remnants of these liche-emperors are then bound within caskets and reliquaries and mounted on the necro-arcane aberrations known as Mortis Engines. Such ghastly conveyances are formed from twisted osseous matter and held aloft by the spirits of those once bound into service by the destroyed Deathmage. They soar through the skies in ominous silence, the steady eye of a hurricane of necromantic energy. Each Mortis Engine acts as a lodestone of Shyishan power, clawing amethyst magic to itself for other practitioners of the black arts to wield. In times of crisis, the Corpsemaster charged with custodianship of the Engine can unleash its stored energies in a single terrible pulse, dragging undead warriors to their feet once more as entire ranks of enemies collapse like a tower of cards in a chill breeze.

Such is the morbid power that surrounds the Mortis Engines that even the predatory spells of the Arcanum Optimar have been known to avoid them; some part of their strange animus recognises the aura of pure ending-magic that clings to these horrific creations and causes them to keep their distance.

BEASTS OF THE GRAVE

It is not only the remains of mortal warriors that can be resurrected through the power of necromancy. Imbued with necrotic energy, hulking monsters and terrifying grave-drakes rise once more to cast their shadow across the land, their predatory instincts still powerful despite the desiccation wrought upon their bodies.

TERRORGHEISTS

Terrorgheists are abominations of the foulest kind, unliving terrors dragged forth from the depths of antiquity. In the lost eras of history, colossal chiropteran predators haunted the skies of the Mortal Realms, preying upon their fellow megafauna and leeching them dry of blood. Many of these leather-winged predators were hunted to extinction or otherwise starved when the spread of civilisation robbed them of their favoured prey. They slunk away into dismal caves and echoing vaults to die, embittered and voracious – and it was these corpses that early practitioners of necromancy discovered and raised as the horrifying Terrorgheists. Their teeth and claws are the length of Sigmarite zweihanders and are capable of cleaving through armour with equal ease, but these monstrous creatures possess an even more fearsome weapon in their arsenal: their infamous killing shriek. As a Terrorgheist hurtles from the sky towards the battlefield, it will unleash a piercing audial barrage, splitting the flesh and pulping the skulls of its prey through sheer sonic pressure. Survivors are left reeling and disoriented, defenceless against the eternally starving beast as it descends upon them and swallows them whole. Even should a Terrorgheist be slain, its threat is not ended: its carcass will writhe and pulsate with dark energies before bursting open, unleashing a cloud of bats from within the beast's atrophied guts to tear at the foe.

Terrorgheists are most commonly associated with the cursed abhorrants of Ushoran, for something in that degenerate vampiric bloodline leads them to find kinship with these foul creatures. However, vampires of more noble stock still seek out Terrorgheist remains to add to their menageries – and not solely for the power they offer in battle. The Terrorgheist has become a feared symbol of Shyish across the realms, an undead alpha-predator that the Soulblight nobility cannot help but admire. Goblets overflowing with fresh blood are still raised in toast to Morbheg, the dreaded father of Terrorgheists, who is said to have supped upon the ichor of godbeasts. More than one dynasty's elaborate coat of arms incorporates

the aspect of the Terrorgheist, but the Khirogarvii of Ghur go one step further. An offshoot of the monstrous Avengorii lineage, these vampires worship every Terrorgheist as a shard of Nagash's black soul, cladding themselves in armour and capes made from their remains in order to better achieve communion with their master.

ZOMBIE DRAGONS

Zombie Dragons are a loathsome sight. What was once a majestic, long-lived king amongst beasts has been twisted and remade through the power of necromancy. Mouldering bone and withered muscle take the place of glistening scales, and the keen intelligence possessed by living dragons is brutally stripped away and replaced entirely with their master's will. Yet though all sane mortals consider them hideous to behold, Zombie Dragons are nevertheless terrifying adversaries. They have lost none of their strength or ferocity; indeed, the necrotic energy that infests them seems only to amplify their hunger. With raking claws and monstrous fangs, they puncture and tear their way through anything not crushed beneath their sheer bulk. A Zombie Dragon's most terrifying weapon, however, is its pestilential breath. What was once a torrent of raging flame now emanates as a seeping, noxious cloud, blistering armour and flesh as those caught in it devolve into withered husks.

The raising of a Zombie Dragon is a crowning achievement for any practitioner of necromancy, and many Soulblight nobles consider these drakes the only creatures worthy of bearing them to war. Such students of the forbidden arts will embark upon long and harrowing quests to legendary draconic boneyards, overcoming punishing trials and battling their way through all manner of strange beasts – to say nothing of the dragons themselves, who consider the violation of their solemn resting places to be an unforgivable insult. Even should they reach their goal, only by working a ritual of vast debasement and sacrifice can these undead champions hope to successfully resurrect a zombified drake and bind it into service. Only a scant few Zombie Dragons, typically those animated by natural wellsprings of necromantic magic, possess even a flicker of sentience; the majority are entirely directed by the will of their master. Should the summoner be slain, the Zombie Dragon will begin to crumble and collapse, its unholy animus dissipating until it can be called forth once more.

THE THRILL OF THE HUNT

Soulblight creatures of all kinds – even the most seemingly mindless – obsess over the notion of the hunt. To many, the act of stalking and feasting upon lesser beings is their unholy birthright; some even fixate on the pursuit itself with a near religious mania, a fascination that is particularly prevalent amongst those dynasties that have long persisted in Ghur. Even the most courtly vampires can be persuaded to indulge their lust for the hunt with only the most minor of urgings, for through such apparently rarefied means, they are able to give some vent to the beast that lurks in the hollow left behind by their soul. To them, the realms are their vast, overrun estates-to-be, the mouldering creatures of the night are their steeds and faithful bloodhounds, and nations of terrified mortals are nothing more than mindless game-beasts to be toyed with at leisure.

Even amongst the ranks of the vampires, there are some hunting parties and fraternities that have achieved particular notoriety. Foremost amongst these is the Crimson Court. A coven of Gravelords drawn from different lineages and led by one of the infamous von Carsteins – at least, so Prince Duvalle himself claims to be – these vampires ape the well-to-do hunting lodges of mortal high society, stalking their carefully chosen victims with a malicious glee before pouncing and gorging upon their blood. Duvalle is a talented warrior and warlock with a wide streak of near unrestrained sadism. He and his fellow courtiers – the hulking and humourless enforcer Gorath von Marusi, the quicksilver duellist Vellas von Faine and the twisted fiend known as Ennias Curse-born – employ a mixture of magical glamours and deathless might to run down their prey and satisfy their fell cravings. Most recently, the Crimson Court has been sighted travelling to the living mountain of Beastgrave, there to seek out new and exhilarating prey.

Not all Soulblight hunting parties choose to prey upon the living. All but the crudest vampires have a respect for antiquity, a quirk of their own unnaturally extended lifespans, and Gravelords of a scholarly persuasion often lead warrior bands or even small armies to sites of ancient splendour in search of relics for their private collections. Such places are often protected by fellow undead. The Mirrored City of Shadespire, one of the most infamous of all such decrepit wonders, is stalked by the Sepulchral Guard – a band of Deathrattle Skeletons whose curse sees them retain a fragment of their former personalities and thus an appreciation for their horrifying existence. Led by the Sepulchral Warden, the former Lord Marshal of the city, they pursue interlopers with a relentless fervour and hack them down with rusted blades.

The forces of the undead are utterly relentless, immune to mortal weaknesses such as fear and hunger. When commanded by their vampiric masters, they can overwhelm even the proudest foe.

COLOURS OF THE GRAVE

The hosts of the Soulblight Gravelords are terrifying to behold, for they advance as a vast tide of rotting, walking dead spearheaded by the charge of mighty vampiric warriors and beasts. Here we present a showcase of Soulblight Gravelords miniatures, painted by the 'Eavy Metal team and the Design Studio army painters.

None are as skilled in the forbidden art of necromancy as Nagash. The Undying King can resurrect entire battalions of undead warriors with but a thought before obliterating his foes with storms of necrotic magic.

Lauka Vai, Mother of Nightmares

Vengorian Lord

Mannfred von Carstein, Mortarch of Night

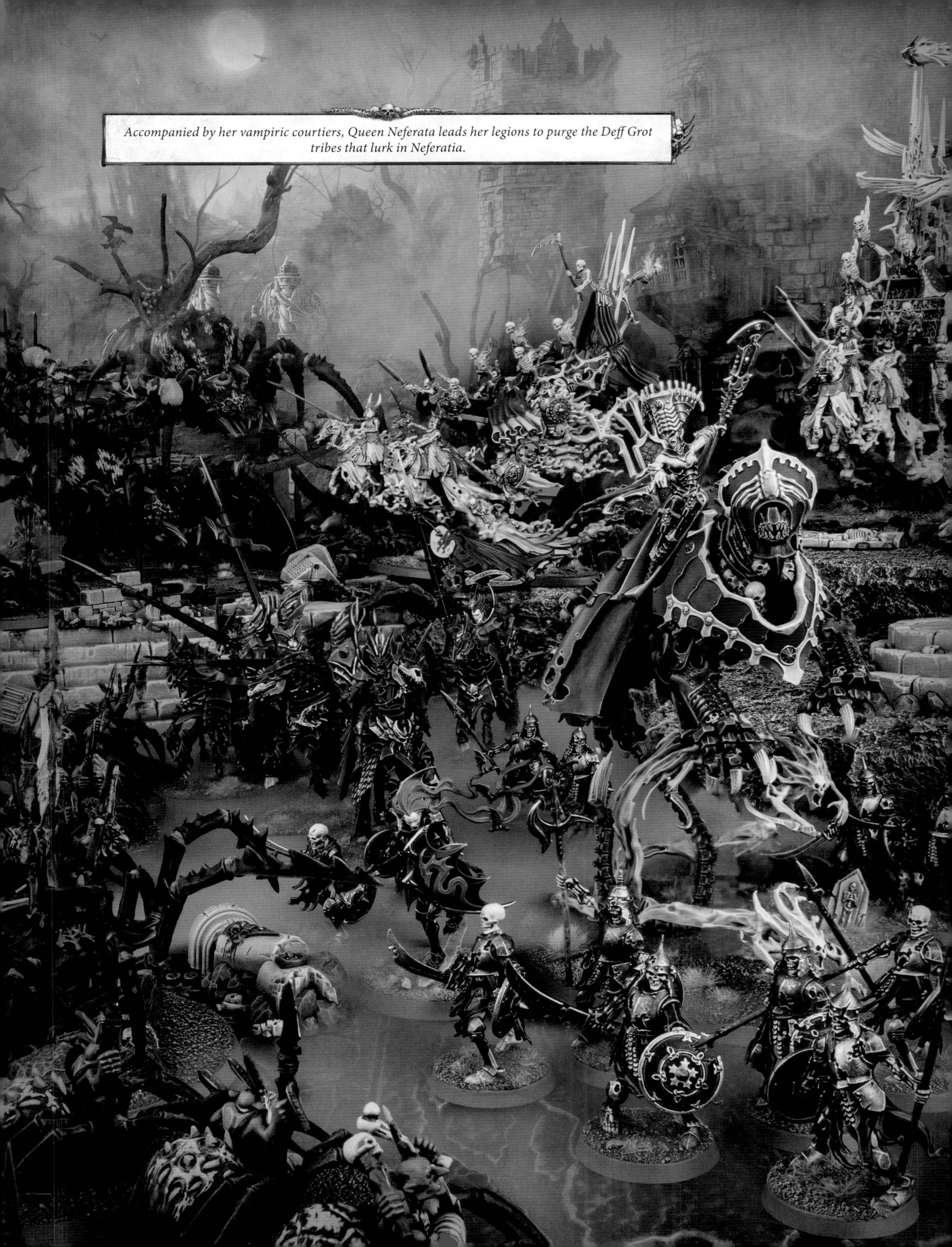

Accompanied by her vampiric courtiers, Queen Neferata leads her legions to purge the Deff Grot tribes that lurk in Neferatia.

Belladamma Volga, First of the Vyrkos

Radukar the Beast

Lady Annika, the Thirsting Blade

Kritza, the Rat Prince

Vampire Lord

The vampires call forth the dead of ancient wars, commanding them to march to battle once more.
The Vyrkos vampires revel in the thrill of pursuit and the bloody slaughter that awaits them at the hunt's end.

Blood Knight

Blood Knight Standard Bearer

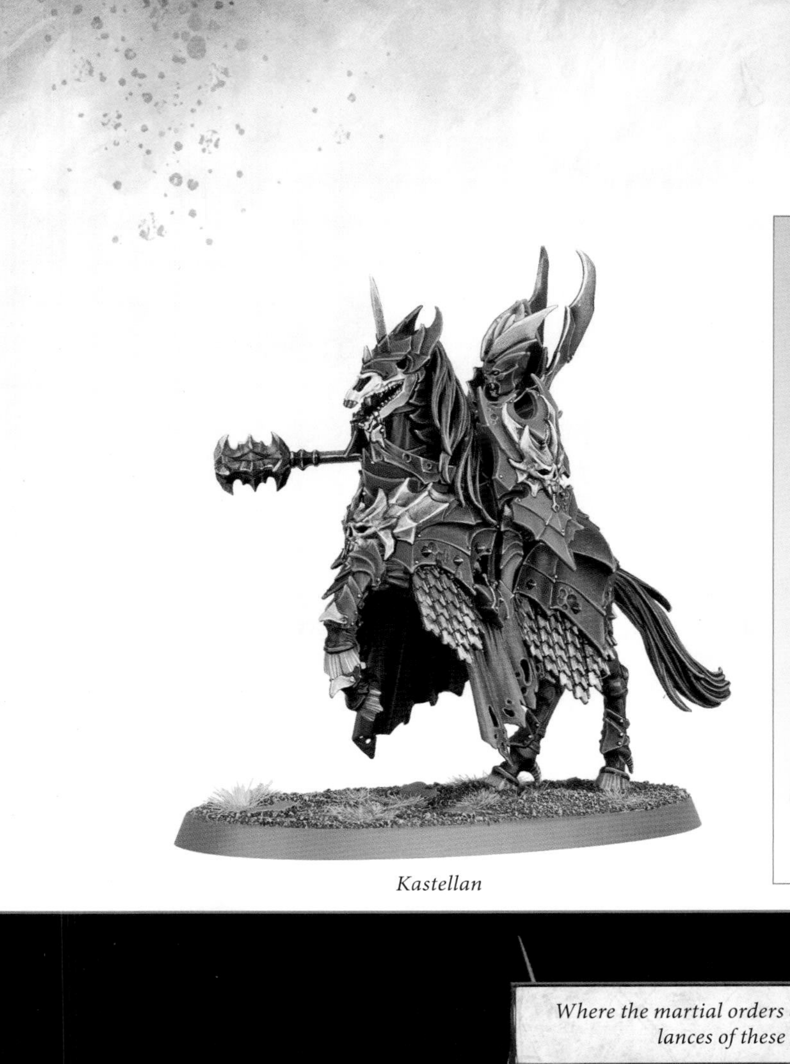

Kastellan

Blood Knight of the Kastelai Dynasty

Where the martial orders of the Blood Knights ride, those who are not brutally spitted upon the lances of these vampiric paragons of war are soon trampled into the dirt.

Skeleton Champion

Deathrattle Skeleton Standard Bearer

Deathrattle Skeletons

Deathrattle Skeletons are clad in the armour of ages past.

A mighty Wight King commands a thrall Necromancer to reinforce his skeletal ranks as the fleshless undead legions march to war.

In the foetid jungles and swamps of Invidia, the forces of the Legion of Night continue to contest the holdings of the Plague Lord's daemons.

Wight King

Black Knight

Fell Bats are as at home swooping through the subterranean caverns of the realms as they are the night sky, falling upon the skaven with piercing shrieks before tearing them asunder and draining their blood.

Fell Bat

Fell Bat

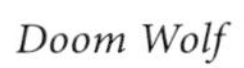

Doom Wolf

Dire Wolf

In the frozen tundras of Carstinia, a haggard and wearied Freeguild company is run to the ground by a pack of Dire Wolves. What follows is sure to be savage in the extreme.

Deadwalker Zombies

Corpse Carts are amongst the foulest creations of the necromantic arts. Where these grim conveyances rattle along, hordes of zombies lurch to their feet, staggering towards the foe with murderous intent.

Radukar and his Thirsting Court rule over the cursed city of Ulfenkarn with a cruel hand, preying upon its dejected inhabitants and relishing any opportunity to destroy those who would lay low their stronghold.

Ennias Curse-born | *Vellas von Faine* | *Prince Duvalle* | *Gorath the Enforcer*

The Crimson Court

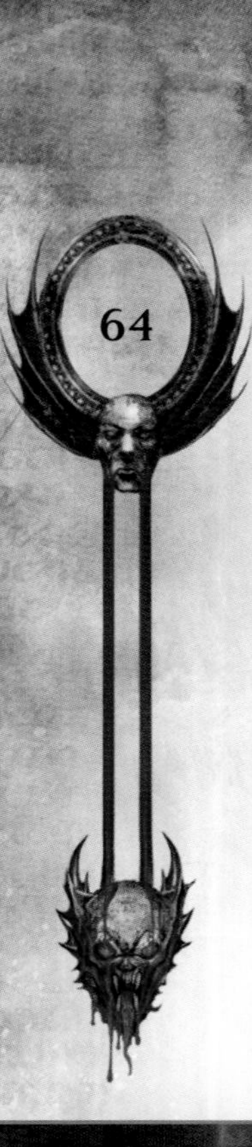

MARCH OF THE LIVING DEAD

To witness the Soulblight Gravelords on the march is to see death itself approaching. The trudging corpse-soldiers are as implacable as they are fearless, while their vampiric masters are themselves formidable warriors. There are many ways to go about assembling these armies of the undead; we have presented one such method below.

The Soulblight Gravelords are one of the most flexible armies in Warhammer Age of Sigmar, combining large units of difficult-to-shift infantry, swift shock troops, terrifying monsters and characters who offer great value in the arenas of combat and magic alike. Considering the breadth of their available units and the many options for tailoring your army through allegiance abilities, it can sometimes be a little overwhelming to know where to start amassing your undead horde. Read on to discover how we put together the force pictured below.

When building an army for a faction with multiple sets of battle traits, it's a good idea to consider which one you favour before beginning. We chose the Legion of Night for this army, since it offered benefits to a lot of the units we wanted to field. Of course, when choosing a general for this legion, one name immediately stands out: Mannfred von Carstein. A superb warrior, wizard and general, Mannfred will both keep our warriors in fighting form and spearhead possibly game-winning charges. No self-respecting Vampire Lord would ever leave their forbidding lair without some minions, and so Mannfred is accompanied by a pair of Wight Kings as well as a Necromancer; the former two characters will add some extra punch to our advances and empower our more skeletal units, while the latter will focus on resurrecting fallen undead and providing another chance to unbind enemy spells. Perhaps if the Necromancer excels, the Mortarch will share some arcane knowledge with him in the aftermath of battle (though, knowing Mannfred, we wouldn't count on it).

Legion of Night armies regularly field sizeable units of infantry to bait their enemies into deadly traps. To represent this, we've included one unit apiece of Deadwalker Zombies, Deathrattle Skeletons and Grave Guard. Though they might not be the most formidable fighters, when they swarm in great numbers, these resurrected warriors can be surprisingly efficient – and, more importantly, by using the Deathly Invocation or Endless Legions battle traits, they can return even after they've been slain. Remember to position some gravesites near objectives, and try to keep at least one **Hero** and one Corpse Cart – out of the two we've selected – near the units likely to take the brunt of the fighting. Few armies are better at waging wars of attrition than yours.

If the Soulblight Gravelords have a weakness, it is their lack of shooting; against more ranged-focused armies, they can be stymied early on, particularly if their vital support characters are targeted. Thankfully, the Legion of Night has a counter to this in its ability to deploy outflanking units. The swifter these are, the better, so we've chosen a pack of Vargheists, some slavering Dire Wolves and a lance of Black Knights. Their job is to tie up enemy ranged units or prey on isolated **Heroes** with all the callousness Mannfred demands. When combined with the relentless infantry advance, the foe will soon find themselves ensnared in our cunning scheme. Keep all this in mind and soon you too will be counted amongst the most dreaded lords of the night!

1. Mannfred von Carstein, Mortarch of Night
2. Wight King on Skeletal Steed
3. Wight King
4. Necromancer
5. Deathrattle Skeletons
6. Deadwalker Zombies
7. Grave Guard
8. Corpse Cart with Unholy Lodestone
9. Corpse Cart with Balefire Brazier
10. Black Knights
11. Dire Wolves
12. Vargheists

'I have fought ten thousand battles, dined on the blood of kings and endured the destruction of entire worlds. And still, there are few finer pleasures to me than when the enemy attempts to run. What can I say? I'm a creature of simple... tastes.'

- Mannfred von Carstein

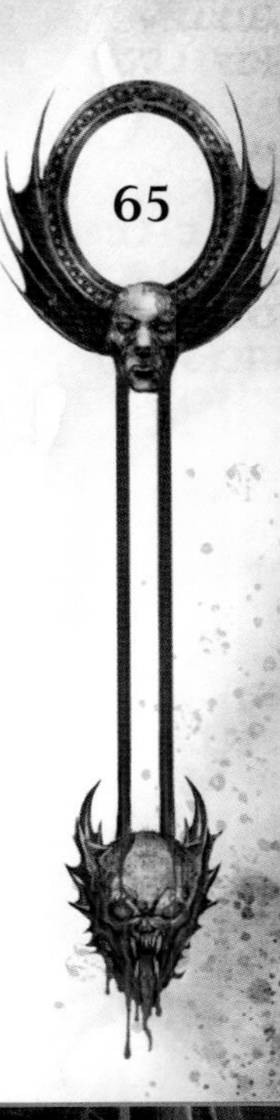

PAINTING YOUR SOULBLIGHT GRAVELORDS

A Soulblight Gravelords collector has an impressive range of Citadel Miniatures to choose from when it comes to building their legions. From lowly companies of skeletons to mighty Zombie Dragons, there's a great variety to tackle with a paintbrush. In this section, you'll find some helpful tips and techniques to get you started.

Few sights are quite as stirring to a collector as a fully painted Citadel Miniature. Whether you're looking to assemble mighty armies ready for the gaming table or choose your favourite models to lavish time and attention on, there's a real satisfaction to be had in adding colour and detail until you have a collection you can be proud of. With their gothic imagery and wide selection of units, the Soulblight Gravelords are a great option for painters of all skill levels. On the following pages, you'll find useful tips from our own cabal of Necromancers (the Design Studio army painters) to get your undead looking their best.

At their core, the Soulblight Gravelords are relatively simple to paint: master some basic techniques for bleached bone, rusted armour and rotting flesh, and you'll have a respectable Battle Ready force in no time! However, for those looking to take their painting to the next level, the Soulblight Gravelords offer plenty of opportunity. Experiment with different methods of painting rust and patination, and you'll surely find something that makes your hordes look like the ancient corpses that they are.

The eponymous Soulblight vampires are each the equivalent of a character in another army, and spending extra time on these blood-drinking champions to really make them pop is well worth it. Looking through compilations of heraldic devices can offer some great inspiration for the sigils of your vampire dynasty, which – once you're confident enough – you can paint on to unit standards or even shields to really mark your collection as your own.

PAINTING GUIDES

The Warhammer YouTube channel is a fantastic source of inspiration and advice for both budding and veteran hobbyists. It offers a range of painting guides for different armies and colour schemes, and explains how to use the Citadel Colour System.

SKELETON ARMOUR

Over a Chaos Black undercoat, basecoat the armour with Iron Warriors.

Apply a shade of Nuln Oil to the armour.

Use several thin coats of Leadbelcher to highlight the raised segments of the armour.

Edge highlight with Stormhost Silver. Add chips and dints by sporadically painting tiny dots and dashes.

SKELETON BONE

Basecoat the bone areas with Morghast Bone.

Over this, apply a coat of Skeleton Horde Contrast paint, being careful not to let it pool.

Layer with Ushabti Bone. As you do so, practise your villainous Necromancer's cackle.

Finish with a careful highlight of Pallid Wych Flesh.

SKELETON BLACK CLOTH

Over a basecoat of Abaddon Black, highlight with Lupercal Green.

Highlight with Sons of Horus Green to intensify the colour.

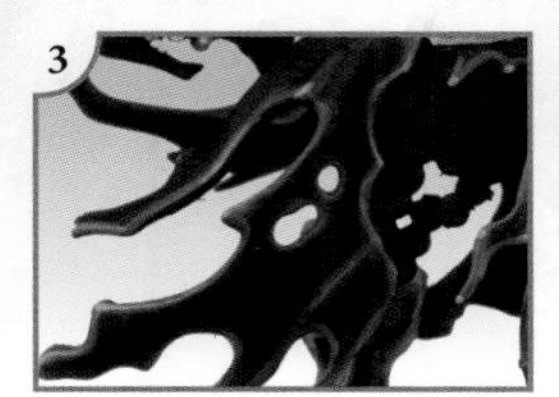
Finally, highlight the more pronounced folds and edges with Administratum Grey.

Lining: Mephiston Red (basecoat), Nuln Oil (shade), Mephiston Red (layer), Evil Sunz Scarlet and Balor Brown (highlights).

SKELETON SHIELD

Field: Basecoat the whole shield with Abaddon Black. Highlight with Incubi Darkness and Thunderhawk Blue.

Trim: Carefully basecoat the trim with Runelord Brass. Shade with Agrax Earthshade and highlight with Runefang Steel.

LEATHER STRAPS

Basecoat with Doombull Brown, shade with Agrax Earthshade, then highlight with Skrag Brown and Balor Brown.

CHAINMAIL

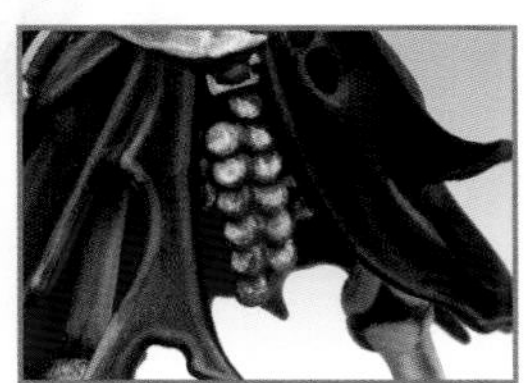
Basecoat with Canoptek Alloy, apply a 1:1 mix of Wyldwood and Contrast Medium, then highlight with Canoptek Alloy and Runefang Steel.

SKELETON BANNER

Field: Khorne Red (basecoat), Nuln Oil (recess shade), Evil Sunz Scarlet and Jokaero Orange (highlights).

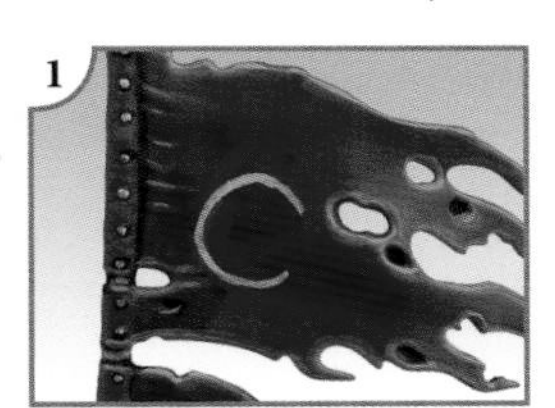
Paint the outline of the crescent shape with thinned Morghast Bone.

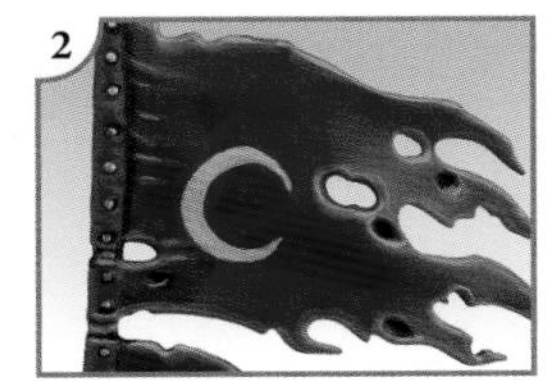
Broaden the crescent with Morghast Bone, cutting back in and tidying up with Khorne Red.

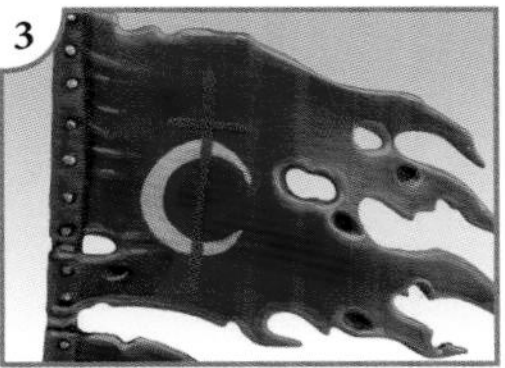
Using Mechanicus Standard Grey, paint a long vertical line down through the crescent and a short horizontal line to create the sword shape.

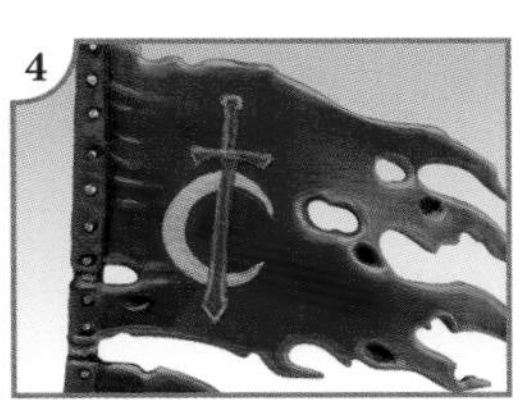
Finalise the shape of the sword with Mechanicus Standard Grey and then apply a highlight of Administratum Grey to add definition.

VAMPIRE FACE

Over a Chaos Black undercoat, basecoat with Rakarth Flesh.

Shade with Reikland Fleshshade, being careful not to be too heavy-handed or to let the paint pool.

Layer with Rakarth Flesh, avoiding the recesses.

Highlight with Pallid Wych Flesh.

Block in the mouth and eyes with Rhinox Hide. For the whites of the eyes and the fangs, use White Scar.

VAMPIRE BLACK ARMOUR

Undercoat the model with Chaos Black spray

Apply a chunky edge highlight of Dark Reaper.

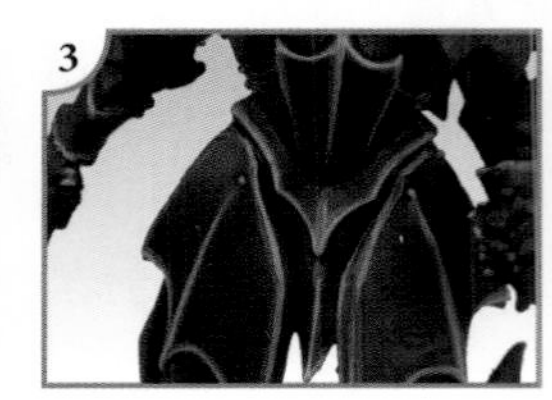

Apply a further edge highlight of Russ Grey.

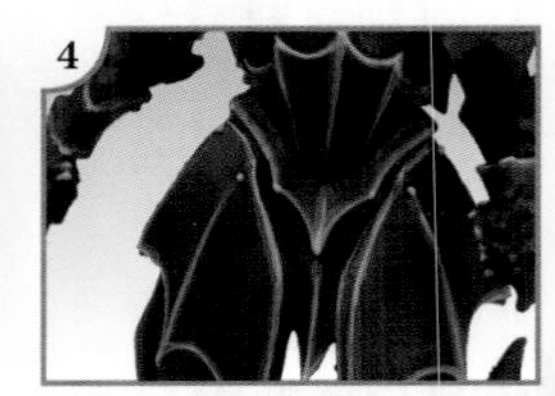

Highlight the angular edges of the armour with Administratum Grey.

DIRE WOLF FUR

Apply a drybrush of Eshin Grey over a Chaos Black undercoat.

Next, drybrush with Stormvermin Fur.

Drybrush with Administratum Grey. To add definition, pick out some of the hairs with the tip of a S Layer brush.

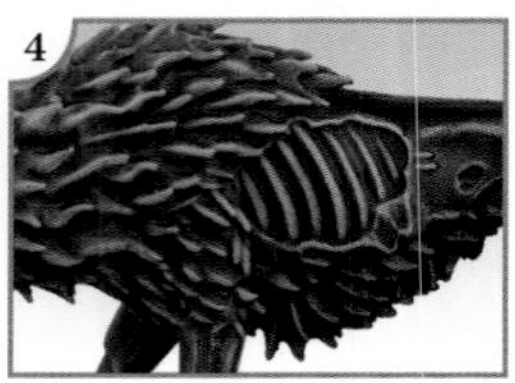

You can then tidy up the smooth areas of skin with Abaddon Black, avoiding the drybrushed parts.

DIRE WOLF DETAILS

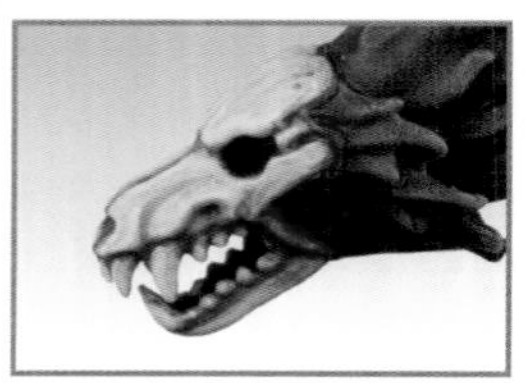

Bone: Ushabti Bone (basecoat), Agrax Earthshade (shade), Screaming Skull (layer), White Scar (highlight).

Exposed Muscle: Wazdakka Red (basecoat), Squig Orange (highlight), Blood For The Blood God (technical).

Eyes: Paint the socket with Abaddon Black. Apply Yriel Yellow to the eyeball followed by a smaller dot of White Scar.
Teeth: Paint using the same method as for Bone.

TOP TIP

It is good practice to apply a coat of Munitorum Varnish spray to protect your models against the wear and tear of battle, making sure to follow the instructions on the can.

Alternatively, if you'd rather add a protective layer by hand, you can apply a coat of Stormshield instead.

VARGHEIST DETAILS

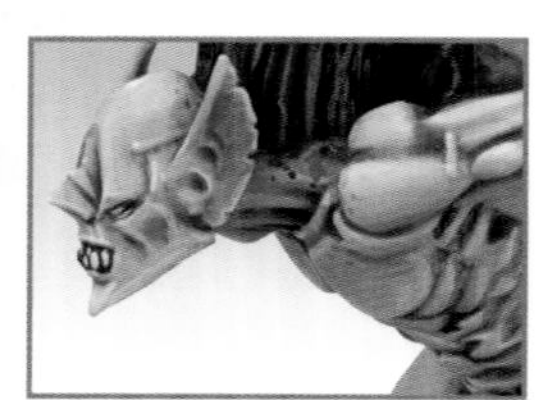

Skin: Rakarth Flesh (basecoat), Agrax Earthshade (recess shade), Rakarth Flesh (layer), Pallid Wych Flesh (highlight).

Hocks: Apply a few coats of Basilicanum Grey, layering more towards the foot, then further darken with Black Templar. Highlight with Stormvermin Fur and Baneblade Brown.

Wings: Cadian Fleshtone (basecoat), 1:1 mix of Agrax Earthshade and Lahmian Medium (shade), Kislev Flesh (drybrush).
Mottling: Black Templar (contrast/ stippling), Baneblade Brown (drybrush).

Fur: Basecoat with Flesh Tearers Red and add Black Templar to the lower half of the mane. Highlight with Wild Rider Red, then highlight with Cadian Fleshtone towards the outer edges.

ZOMBIE PALE FLESH

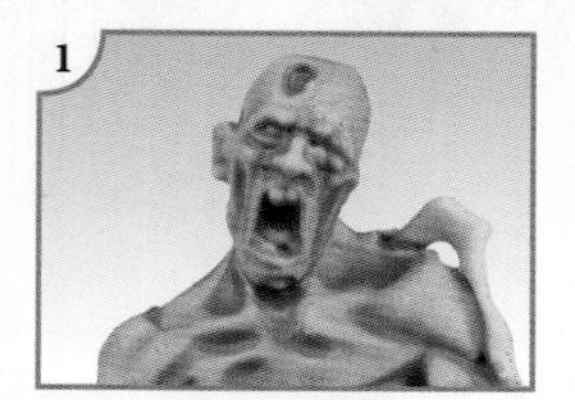

Over a Grey Seer basecoat, apply a 1:2 mix of Gorthor Brown and Lahmian Medium to the flesh.

Layer the flesh with Karak Stone, making sure to avoid the recesses.

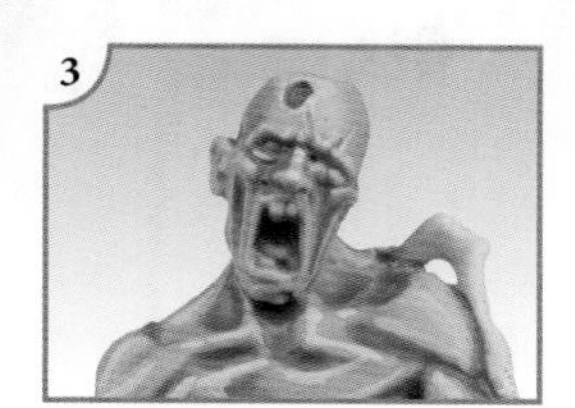

Highlight with Ionrach Skin.

Apply Rhinox Hide to the eyes and mouth. Add Grey Seer to the eyes, Ushabti Bone to the teeth and Pink Horror to the tongue.

ZOMBIE FLESH VARIANTS

Rotting Flesh: Grey Seer (basecoat), Militarum Green (contrast), Baneblade Brown and Karak Stone (highlights).

Dark Flesh: Dryad Bark (basecoat), Nuln Oil (shade), Steel Legion Drab and Karak Stone (highlights).

ZOMBIE HAIR

Greying Hair: Grey Seer (basecoat), Wyldwood (contrast), Stormvermin Fur (layer), Administratum Grey (highlight).

Light Hair: Morghast Bone (basecoat), Seraphim Sepia (shade), Ushabti Bone (highlight).

ZOMBIE CLOTH

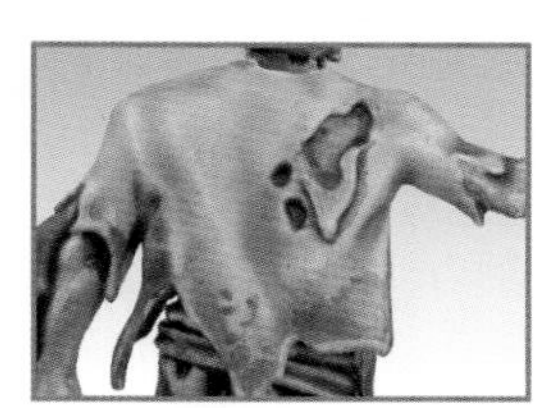

Grey Cloth: Grey Seer (basecoat), Space Wolves Grey (contrast), Grey Seer (highlight).

Off-white Cloth: Grey Seer (basecoat), 1:3 mix of Stormvermin Fur and Contrast Medium (shade), Pallid Wych Flesh (highlight).

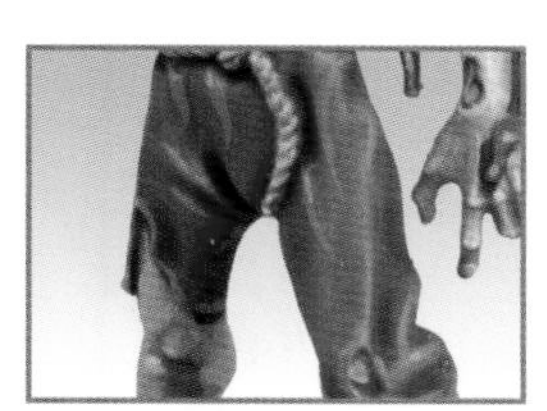

Red Cloth: Wazdakka Red (basecoat), Agrax Earthshade (shade), Tuskgor Fur and Karak Stone (highlights).

TOP TIP

Stipple thinned browns towards the bottoms of trousers and dresses to give the impression of mud-soaked and dirt-encrusted cloth. You can use Contrast, Shade, Base or Layer paints for this; just remember that less is more and that it's best to build up colour with a couple of thin layers.

FELL BAT DETAILS

Wings: Chaos Black (undercoat), Skavenblight Dinge (drybrush), Stormvermin Fur (drybrush/highlight), Baneblade Brown (highlight).

Fur: Chaos Black (undercoat), Skavenblight Dinge (drybrush), Baneblade Brown (drybrush).

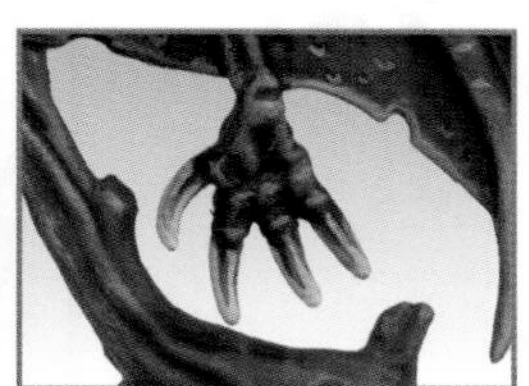

Claws: Basecoat the claws with Rhinox Hide. Apply XV-88 in lines to represent striations. Highlight with Ushabti Bone.

Skin: Knight-Questor Flesh (basecoat), Agrax Earthshade (shade), Knight-Questor Flesh (layer), Karak Stone (highlight).
Teeth and Eyes: Pallid Wych Flesh.

BLOOD KNIGHTS ARMOUR

Over a Chaos Black undercoat, basecoat with Mephiston Red.

Shade the armour with Nuln Oil.

Layer with Evil Sunz Scarlet, leaving the recesses dark.

Apply a fine highlight of Fire Dragon Bright to the edges of the armour.

BLOOD KNIGHTS BARDING

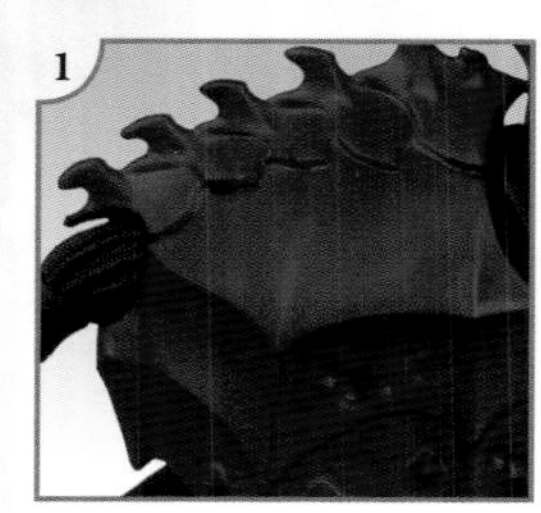

Basecoat with Gal Vorbak Red.

Apply slightly thinned Black Templar to the recesses.

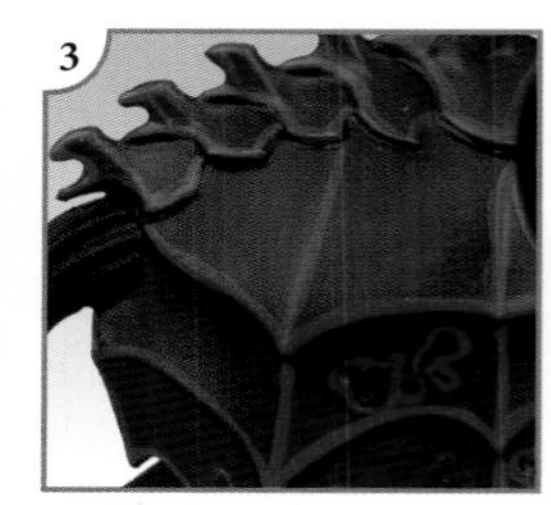

Highlight with Mephiston Red.

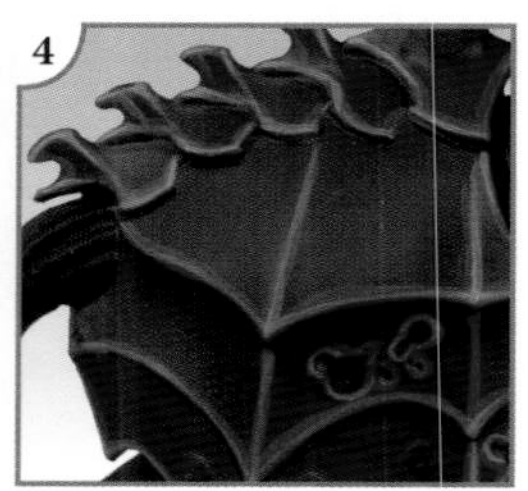

Apply a final highlight of Wild Rider Red.

BLOOD KNIGHT BARDING CLOTH

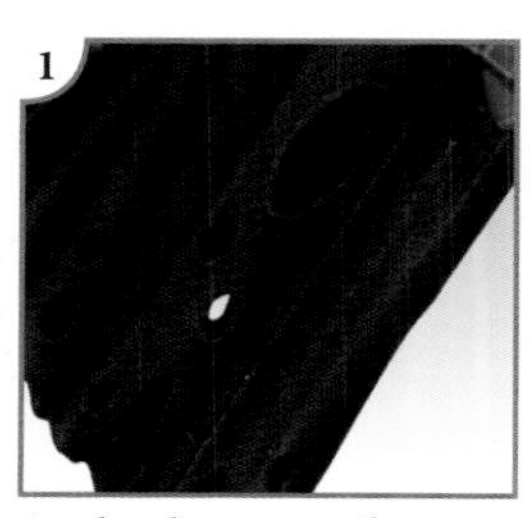

Apply a basecoat of Abaddon Black.

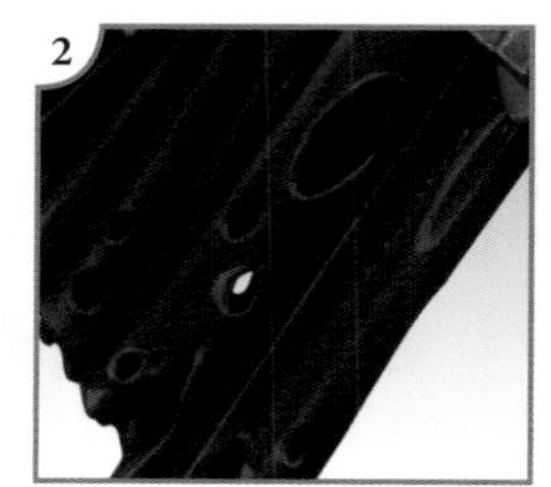

Add a chunky highlight of Lupercal Green to the edges of the cloth.

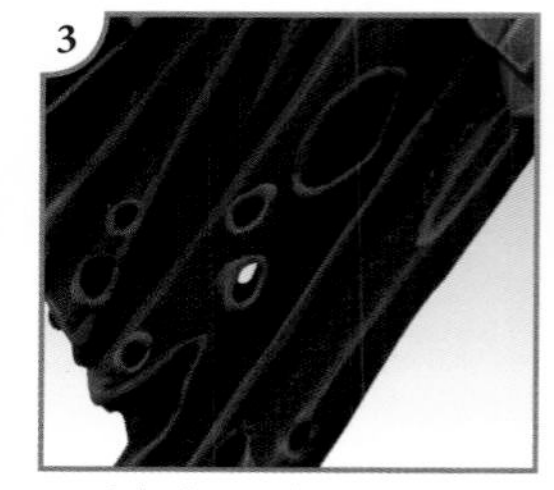

Highlight with a thin line of Sons of Horus Green, using a smaller brush.

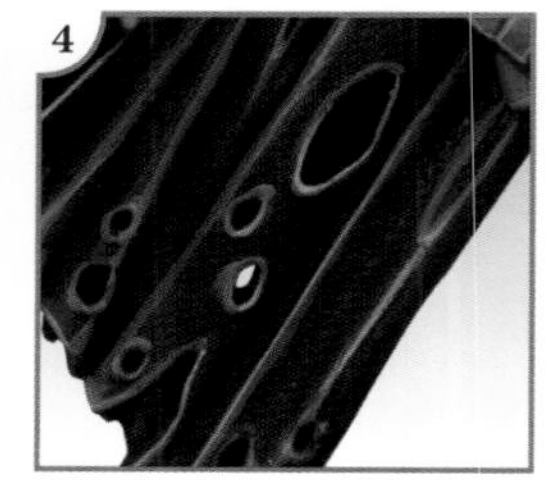

Finally, highlight the most prominent edges with Administratum Grey.

NIGHTMARE DETAILS

Hide: Abaddon Black (basecoat), Skavenblight Dinge and Gorthor Brown (highlights).

Mane: Skavenblight Dinge (basecoat), Agrax Earthshade (shade), Stormvermin Fur and Karak Stone (highlights).

Hooves: After basecoating with Stormvermin Fur, paint Karak Stone in downward lines to create striations.

Skull: Ushabti Bone (basecoat), Agrax Earthshade (shade), Ushabti Bone (layer), Pallid Wych Flesh (highlight).

VYRKOS DYNASTY DETAILS

Pelt: Grey Seer (basecoat), Apothecary White (contrast), 1:1 mix of Basilicanum Grey/Contrast Medium (recess shade), White Scar (highlight).

Green Cloth: Lupercal Green (basecoat), Loren Forest (layer), Straken Green and Karak Stone (edge highlights).

Burgundy Cloth: Barak-Nar Burgundy (basecoat), Nuln Oil (shade), Daemonette Hide (layer), Slaanesh Grey (highlight).

Blood Markings: Mix Mephiston Red and Khorne Red to a ratio of 1:1. Paint thin lines first, then broaden to a stretched triangle shape.

KASTELAI DYNASTY DETAILS

Armour: Leadbelcher (basecoat), Nuln Oil (shade), Leadbelcher (layer), Stormhost Silver (edge highlight).

Barding: Iron Warriors (basecoat), 1:3 mix of Wyldwood and Contrast Medium (shade), Leadbelcher (edges), Stormhost Silver (angles).

Red Cloth: Khorne Red (basecoat), Nuln Oil (shade), Khorne Red (layer).

Shield: Abaddon Black (basecoat), Mechanicus Standard Grey (edge highlight), Administratum Grey (angle highlight).

Purple Cloth: Xereus Purple (basecoat), Nuln Oil (shade), Genestealer Purple and Emperor's Children (edge highlights).

Helmet: Mephiston Red (basecoat), Nuln Oil (shade), Evil Sunz Scarlet (highlight), Fire Dragon Bright (edge highlight).

Brass: Runelord Brass (basecoat), Cryptek Armourshade (shade), Runelord Brass (layer), Stormhost Silver (edge highlight).

For a verdigris effect, apply small patches and dribbles of Nihilakh Oxide, taking a 'less is more' approach.

TOP TIP

Skulls are a great addition to any Soulblight Gravelords base. To paint your skulls, you can follow the same method as for Skeleton Bone (pg 66).

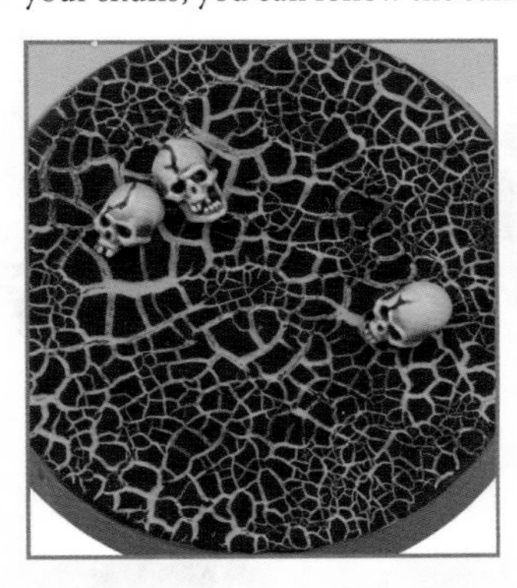

Apply a basecoat of Grey Seer, then coat with Nihilakh Oxide. Once dry, apply a thick coat of Mordant Earth (it might be a good idea to experiment on some spare bases first). Finally, paint the base rim with Stormvermin Fur.

Start by applying a coat of Stirland Mud. Once dry, drybrush with Balor Brown and Ushabti Bone. Add Middenland Tufts and patches of Valhallan Blizzard. Once dry, add some splashes of Blood For The Blood God. Finally, paint the base rim with Steel Legion Drab.

THE SOULBLIGHT GRAVELORDS

This battletome contains all of the rules you need to field your Soulblight Gravelords miniatures on the battlefields of the Mortal Realms, from a host of exciting allegiance abilities to a range of warscrolls and warscroll battalions. The rules are split into the following sections:

ALLEGIANCE ABILITIES
This section describes the allegiance abilities available to a Soulblight Gravelords army. The rules for using allegiance abilities can be found in the *Warhammer Age of Sigmar Core Book*.

SOULBLIGHT GRAVELORDS
Allegiance abilities available to all Soulblight Gravelords armies (pg 72-73).

THE CURSED BLOODLINES
Additional allegiance abilities available to Soulblight Gravelords armies that have been given the appropriate keyword by the Cursed Bloodlines battle trait (pg 74-83).

SPELL LORES
Spells available to **WIZARDS** in a Soulblight Gravelords army (pg 84-85).

BATTLEPLAN
This section includes a new narrative battleplan that can be played with a Soulblight Gravelords army (pg 86-87).

PATH TO GLORY
This section contains rules for using your Soulblight Gravelords collection in Path to Glory campaigns (pg 88-92).

WARSCROLLS
This section includes all of the warscrolls you will need to play games of Warhammer Age of Sigmar with your Soulblight Gravelords miniatures. The following types of warscroll are included in this section:

WARSCROLL BATTALIONS
These are formations made up of several Soulblight Gravelords units that combine their strengths to gain powerful new abilities (pg 94-97).

WARSCROLLS
A warscroll for each unit is included here. The rules for using a Soulblight Gravelords unit, along with its characteristics and abilities, are detailed on its warscroll (pg 98-127).

PITCHED BATTLE PROFILES
This section contains Pitched Battle profiles for the units and warscroll battalions in this book (pg 128).

ALLIES
This section has a list of the allies a Soulblight Gravelords army can include (pg 128).

ALLEGIANCE ABILITIES

SOULBLIGHT GRAVELORDS

BATTLE TRAITS - MASTERS OF DEATH

THE CURSED BLOODLINES
The greatest Soulblight dynasties and legions are mighty beyond measure.

When you choose a Soulblight Gravelords army, you must give it a lineage keyword from the list below. All **SOULBLIGHT GRAVELORDS** units in your army gain that keyword, and you can use the allegiance abilities listed for that dynasty or legion on the pages indicated.

- **LEGION OF BLOOD** (pg 74-75)
- **LEGION OF NIGHT** (pg 76-77)
- **VYRKOS DYNASTY** (pg 78-79)
- **KASTELAI DYNASTY** (pg 80-81)
- **AVENGORII DYNASTY** (pg 82-83)

If a unit already has a lineage keyword on its warscroll, it cannot gain another one. This does not preclude you from including the unit in your army, but you cannot use the allegiance abilities for its dynasty or legion.

SUPREME LORD OF THE UNDEAD
Nagash stands at the apex of the necromantic hierarchy.

You can include **NAGASH** in a Soulblight Gravelords army even though he does not have the **SOULBLIGHT GRAVELORDS** keyword on his warscroll. If you do so, he gains the **SOULBLIGHT GRAVELORDS** keyword on his warscroll and he is treated as a general in addition to the model that is chosen to be the army general, but you cannot include any mercenary units in your army.

THE UNQUIET DEAD

At the bidding of their masters, the undead rise from their graves, balefire eyes blazing with dark purpose.

After territories have been chosen but before armies are set up, you can pick up to 2 points within your territory and up to 2 points anywhere on the battlefield outside your territory to be gravesites. Each gravesite must be more than 1" from all terrain features and objectives.

Instead of setting up a **Soulblight Gravelords Summonable** unit on the battlefield before the battle begins, you can place it to one side and say that it is set up in the grave as a reserve unit. You can set up 1 reserve unit in the grave for each unit you have already set up on the battlefield.

At the end of any of your movement phases, you can set up 1 or more of these units on the battlefield wholly within 12" of a gravesite and more than 9" from all enemy units. At the start of the fourth battle round, reserve units that are still in the grave are destroyed.

LOCUS OF SHYISH

The magical power of Shyish is as relentless as those who wield it.

If the unmodified casting roll for a friendly **Soulblight Gravelords Wizard** attempting to cast a spell from the Lore of the Deathmages or the Lore of the Vampires is 9+ and that spell is not unbound, after the effects of that spell have been resolved, you can immediately resolve the effects of that spell for a second time.

DEATHLESS MINIONS

The undead minions of the Gravelords are oblivious to injury and push forward, unfazed by any resistance.

Roll a dice each time you allocate a wound or mortal wound to a friendly **Soulblight Gravelords** unit wholly within 12" of a friendly **Soulblight Gravelords Hero** or gravesite. On a 6+, that wound or mortal wound is negated.

REANIMATED HORRORS

To face the armies of the Gravelords is to confront the end that awaits all life, a feat beyond most mortals.

Subtract 1 from the Bravery characteristic of enemy units while they are within 6" of 1 friendly **Soulblight Gravelords Deadwalkers** or **Soulblight Gravelords Deathrattle** unit. Subtract 2 from the Bravery characteristic of enemy units instead of 1 while they are within 6" of 2 or more friendly **Soulblight Gravelords Deadwalkers** or **Soulblight Gravelords Deathrattle** units. **Death** units are not affected by this ability.

ENDLESS LEGIONS

Across the realms, charnel pits and mass graves blight the land. The Gravelords wield the corpses within as a weapon, returning them to unlife to serve their will.

At the end of your battleshock phase, count the number of enemy units that were destroyed during that turn and roll a dice, adding the number of destroyed enemy units to the roll. On a 5+, you can pick 1 friendly **Soulblight Gravelords Summonable Deadwalkers** or **Soulblight Gravelords Summonable Deathrattle** unit in your army that has been destroyed. If you do so, a new replacement unit with half the number of models in the unit that was destroyed (rounding up) is added to your army. Set up that unit wholly within 12" of a gravesite and more than 9" from all enemy units.

DEATHLY INVOCATION

Powerful practitioners of death magic are able to summon forth hordes of undead minions in battle.

At the start of your hero phase, you can pick a number of different friendly **Soulblight Gravelords Summonable** units wholly within 12" of a friendly **Soulblight Gravelords Hero** to be affected by a deathly invocation. The number of different friendly **Soulblight Gravelords Summonable** units you can pick is determined by the keyword on that **Hero**'s warscroll:

KEYWORD	NUMBER OF UNITS
Mortarch	up to 4
Vampire	up to 3
Deathmages	up to 2
Deathrattle	up to 2

If the **Hero** has more than 1 of the above keywords on its warscroll, choose 1 of them.

For each of the units you picked, you can heal up to D3 wounds allocated to that unit or, if no wounds are allocated to it, you can return a number of slain models to that unit that have a combined Wounds characteristic of D3 or less. Roll separately for each unit. The same unit cannot benefit from this ability more than once per turn. In addition, a unit cannot benefit from this ability and the Invocation of Nagash ability (pg 98) in the same turn.

Designer's Note: *Some Soulblight Gravelords abilities and spells allow you to return slain models to a unit. When you do so, set up the models one at a time within 1" of a model from their unit that was not returned to the unit earlier in the phase. Slain models can only be set up within 3" of an enemy unit if a model in the unit they are returning to that was not already returned in the same phase is already within 3" of that enemy unit.*

LEGION OF BLOOD

BATTLE TRAITS - A GRIM MAJESTY

IMMORTAL MAJESTY

When Neferata's armies march out to accomplish her designs, they do so in such macabre splendour that the living cannot help but quail before them.

If an enemy unit fails a battleshock test within 3" of any friendly **Legion of Blood Vampire** units, add D3 to the number of models that flee.

FAVOURED RETAINERS

Deathrattle legions are favoured tools of the Legion of Blood, and they enact their masters' plots with unfeeling dedication.

Ignore negative modifiers to hit and wound rolls for attacks made with melee weapons by friendly **Legion of Blood Deathrattle** units while they are wholly within 12" of a friendly **Legion of Blood Vampire** unit or wholly within 18" of a friendly **Legion of Blood Vampire Hero** that is a general.

COMMAND TRAITS - INSTRUMENTS OF NEFERATA'S WILL

Legion of Blood general only.

D6 Command Trait

1 **Premeditated Violence:** *This general has extensively taken the measure of their foes and knows just where to strike for maximum effect.*

If the unmodified hit roll for an attack made with a melee weapon by this general is 6, that attack scores 2 hits on the target instead of 1. Make a wound and save roll for each hit.

2 **Soul-crushing Contempt:** *This coldly regal lord of the dead seeks to break their enemy's bodies and spirits alike.*

Subtract 1 from the Bravery characteristic of enemy units while they are within 3" of this general.

3 **Aristocracy of Blood:** *This general is one of Neferata's favoured agents and shares their mistress's appreciation of precision.*

You can re-roll charge rolls for friendly **Legion of Blood** units while they are wholly within 12" of this general.

4 **Aura of Dark Majesty:** *The beguiling aura that swathes this general can leave an enemy's blade slack and aimless in their grip.*

Subtract 1 from hit rolls for attacks made with melee weapons that target this general.

5 **Walking Death:** *This warrior serves as one of the Mortarch's champions and is a sublimely lethal combatant at close quarters.*

If the unmodified wound roll for an attack made with a melee weapon by this general is 6, that attack inflicts a number of mortal wounds equal to the Damage characteristic of the weapon used for the attack and the attack sequence ends (do not make a save roll).

6 **Sanguine Blur:** *By the time this general's foes have observed the crimson streak heading towards them, it is far too late.*

Friendly units that start a pile-in move wholly within 12" of this general can move an extra 3" when they pile in.

ARTEFACTS OF POWER - TREASURES OF THE BLOODY COURT

Legion of Blood Hero only.

D6	Artefact of Power

1. **Ring of Dominion:** *The faceted crimson gem upon this ring contains the blood of an ancient vampire. Its magic can dominate the minds of lesser beings.*

   Each time the bearer is picked to fight in the combat phase, you can pick 1 enemy model within 3" of the bearer and roll a dice. On a 5+, pick 1 of that model's melee weapons. That model's unit suffers a number of mortal wounds equal to the Damage characteristic of the weapon you picked. You cannot pick a melee weapon that refers to a damage table or ability to determine its damage.

2. **Shadeglass Decanter:** *This cursed vessel siphons away the souls of the living, capturing them forever.*

   After armies have been set up but before the first battle round begins, you can pick 1 enemy **Hero** on the battlefield. In your hero phase, if the bearer and that **Hero** are on the battlefield, you can roll a dice. If the roll is equal to or greater than the number of the current battle round, that **Hero** suffers 1 mortal wound.

3. **Orb of Enchantment:** *To glance into the swirling depths of this crystal orb is to become hypnotised by alluring visions and half-glimpsed futures.*

   Once per battle, at the start of the combat phase, you can pick 1 enemy **Hero** within 3" of the bearer and roll a dice. On a 3+, that **Hero** cannot be picked to fight in that phase.

4. **Soulbound Garments:** *Woven with dark magic, these richly embroidered clothes are as tough as steel plate.*

   Add 1 to save rolls for attacks that target the bearer.

5. **Oubliette Arcana:** *This casket resembles a miniature coffin carved from ivory and black wood. It captures arcane energy, allowing the bearer to redirect an enemy wizard's magic.*

   Once per enemy hero phase, when an enemy **Wizard** successfully casts a spell within 18" of the bearer and that spell is not unbound (even if a friendly **Wizard** attempted to unbind the spell), before resolving the effects of that spell, you can roll a dice. On a 5+, that spell is unbound.

6. **Amulet of Screams:** *The bearer of this amulet can flood the foe's mind with the tormented howling of damned souls, leaving them exposed to their sorcery.*

   Once per battle, when an enemy **Wizard** successfully casts a spell that is not unbound, you can say that the bearer will use their Amulet of Screams. If you do so, that **Wizard** suffers D3 mortal wounds after the effects of that spell have been resolved.

LEGION OF NIGHT

BATTLE TRAITS - IMMORTAL EVIL

THE BAIT

When the Legion of Night marches to war, rank upon rank of deathless warriors are raised to do the commanders' bidding. These silent revenants are expected to draw the wrath of the enemy onto them, enduring long enough for the vampires to strike.

Add 1 to save rolls for attacks that target friendly **LEGION OF NIGHT DEATHRATTLE** and friendly **LEGION OF NIGHT DEADWALKERS** units in the first battle round.

AGELESS CUNNING

Mannfred von Carstein and his minions are creatures of immortal cunning and cruel opportunism. Upon scenting weakness, they will strike from an unexpected angle, emerging from a pall of midnight to lay waste to their unprepared foes.

Instead of setting up a **LEGION OF NIGHT** unit on the battlefield, you can place it to one side and say that it is set up in ambush as a reserve unit. You can set up 1 reserve unit in ambush for each unit you have already set up on the battlefield.

At the end of any of your movement phases, you can set up 1 or more of these units on the battlefield wholly within 6" of the battlefield edge and more than 9" from all enemy units. At the start of the fourth battle round, reserve units that are still in ambush are destroyed.

COMMAND TRAITS - RULERS OF THE NIGHT

LEGION OF NIGHT general only.

D6 Command Trait

1 Above Suspicion: *This general is almost trusted by the Mortarch of Night and given greater leniency for enacting their cunning schemes.*

If this general is set up in ambush using the Ageless Cunning battle trait above, at the end of your movement phase, you can set up this general anywhere on the battlefield more than 9" from all enemy units, instead of wholly within 6" of the battlefield edge.

2 Swift Form: *Whether transforming into a bestial creature or dissipating into dark mist, this general can cover ground with terrible swiftness.*

Add 2 to run and charge rolls for this general.

3 Unbending Will: *This general's sheer willpower is enough to keep their minions animated.*

Do not take battleshock tests for friendly **LEGION OF NIGHT** units while they are wholly within 12" of this general.

4 Merciless Hunter: *The only victory for this general is the complete obliteration of their foe.*

Add 1 to wound rolls for attacks made with melee weapons by this general.

5 Unholy Impetus: *As this general indulges their bloodthirst, the souls of the freshly slain are used to empower the undead hordes.*

In the combat phase, if any enemy models are slain by attacks made with melee weapons by this general in that phase, add 1 to the Attacks characteristic of melee weapons used by friendly **LEGION OF NIGHT** units wholly within 12" of this general until the end of that phase.

6 Terrifying Visage: *This general is a true lord of the night, and more than one foe has been stricken with dread merely upon looking at them.*

Subtract 1 from wound rolls for attacks made with melee weapons that target this general.

ARTEFACTS OF POWER - THE VAULTS OF CARSTINIA

LEGION OF NIGHT HERO only.

D6 Artefact of Power

1 Vial of Pure Blood: *A vial of blood drained from the most pious or righteous mortals can greatly invigorate a creature of the night.*

Once per battle, in your hero phase, you can say that the bearer will drink from their vial of pure blood. If you do so, add 1 to hit and wound rolls for attacks made with melee weapons by the bearer until your next hero phase.

2 Shard of Night: *This black leather brigandine was crafted from the hide of an Abyssal Stalker and grants the wearer that creature's shadowy aura.*

Ignore the Rend characteristic of missile weapons when making save rolls for attacks that target the bearer.

3 Gem of Exsanguination: *This crimson stone pulses hungrily. It craves fresh blood, and its magic is strong enough to burst the arteries of its victims, greedily siphoning their vitae in a tempest of gore.*

Once per battle, at the start of the combat phase, you can pick 1 enemy unit within 6" of the bearer and roll a dice. On a 1, nothing happens. On a 2-5, that unit suffers D3 mortal wounds. On a 6, the unit suffers D6 mortal wounds.

4 Chiropteran Cloak: *This bat-winged cloak is covered with razor-sharp claws. Feasting upon blood drives it into a frenzy, causing it to lash and tear at nearby foes.*

If the unmodified hit roll for an attack made with a melee weapon that targets the bearer is 1, the attacking unit suffers 1 mortal wound after all of its attacks have been resolved.

5 Morbheg's Claw: *This blackened talon is said to belong to Morbheg, father of Terrorgheists.*

In your hero phase, you can say that the bearer will carve sigils into the ground using Morbheg's claw. If you do so, add 2 to casting rolls for friendly LEGION OF NIGHT WIZARDS wholly within 12" of the bearer until your next hero phase. However, the bearer cannot make a normal move, make a charge move, shoot or fight until your next hero phase.

6 Curseblade: *This cursed blade is destined to feast upon the soul of a particular foe.*

After armies have been set up but before the first battle round begins, you can pick 1 enemy HERO on the battlefield. In your hero phase, if the bearer and that HERO are on the battlefield, roll a dice. On a 5+, that HERO suffers 1 mortal wound and you can heal 1 wound allocated to the bearer.

VYRKOS DYNASTY

BATTLE TRAITS - THE BEAST WITHIN

THE STRENGTH OF THE PACK IS THE WOLF

Even the risen dead wielded by Vyrkos vampires seem filled with a hunter's instinct, each warrior working in concert with their masters to encircle and hack apart the prey.

Add 1 to wound rolls for attacks made with melee weapons by friendly **Vyrkos Dynasty Deathrattle** and **Vyrkos Dynasty Deadwalkers** units while they are wholly within 9" of any friendly **Vyrkos Dynasty Vampire Heroes**.

THE STRENGTH OF THE WOLF IS THE PACK

Vyrkos vampires draw strength from the animalistic curse running through their veins, a curse that seems to be magnified in the presence of their kin.

You can re-roll casting rolls for friendly **Vyrkos Dynasty Vampire Wizards**.

COMMAND TRAITS - ALPHA PREDATORS

Vyrkos Dynasty general only.

D6 Command Trait

1 Pack Alpha: *This warrior demonstrates their right to rule through sheer violence.*

Once per turn, this general can use a command ability without a command point being spent.

2 Driven by Deathstench: *This general's predatory instincts have infused into their kin, driving them on with terrifying ferocity.*

You can re-roll charge rolls for friendly **Vyrkos Dynasty** units wholly within 9" of this general.

3 Kin of the Wolf: *Letting out a lupine howl, this general summons packs of undead wolves to the field.*

Once per battle, at the end of your movement phase, you can say that this general will summon a pack of Dire Wolves to the battlefield. If you do so, you can add 1 unit of up to 5 **Dire Wolves** to your army. Set up that unit wholly within 9" of this general and more than 9" from all enemy units.

4 Hunter's Snare: *Like a wolf prowling at the edge of the firelight, this general bides their time awaiting the perfect opportunity to strike.*

If this general contests an objective, the number of models this general counts as is equal to their Wounds characteristic.

5 Spoor Trackers: *So potent is this general's bestial soul that even shambling Deadwalkers act with increased haste in their presence.*

At the start of your hero phase, friendly **Vyrkos Dynasty Deadwalkers** units wholly within 9" of this general can make a normal move of up to 3" (they cannot run).

6 United by Blood: *This general has a curious connection with their mystical blood-curse.*

This general can attempt to unbind 1 spell in the enemy hero phase in the same manner as a **Wizard**. If this general is already a **Wizard**, they can attempt to unbind 1 extra spell in the enemy hero phase.

ARTEFACTS OF POWER - TROPHIES OF THE HUNT

VYRKOS DYNASTY HERO only.

D6	Artefact of Power
1	**Ulfenkarnian Phylactery:** *Crafted by the chamberlain Torgillius, these items allow the bearer's minions to shrug off even terminal blows.* Friendly **SOULBLIGHT GRAVELORDS** units are affected by the Deathless Minions battle trait (pg 73) while they are wholly within 18" of the bearer instead of 12".
2	**Cloak of the Night Prowler:** *Currently considered high fashion amongst Ulfenkarn's vampiric nobility, these mist-swathed capes allow the wearer to seemingly disappear right before an onlooker's eyes.* The bearer can pile in an extra 3" when they make a pile-in move.
3	**Sangsyron:** *This fabled sword is said to possess its own evil animus. Though it has betrayed more than one vampire, should its will be matched by one of equal strength, it will rend and slay with unmatched ferocity.* Pick 1 of the bearer's melee weapons. If the bearer made a charge move in the same turn, add D3 to the Attacks characteristic of that weapon until the end of that turn.
4	**Vilnas' Fang:** *Said to be taken from the legendary twin-headed wolf slain by Radukar, this curved tooth grants the bearer the cunning of a lupine pack and sees them stalk their foes with peerless stealth.* Once per battle, in your charge phase, you can say that the bearer will be imbued with Vilnas' stealth. If you do so, until the end of that phase, add 1 to charge rolls for the bearer for each other friendly **VYRKOS DYNASTY VAMPIRE HERO** on the battlefield.
5	**Terminus Clock:** *Crafted by a mad clockwright of Ulfenkarn, this bizarre cogwork piece ticks without rhyme or reason. Whenever its eclectic count ends, however, the power of magic seems to deaden across the field.* Once per battle, at the start of the enemy hero phase, you can say that the bearer will stop the Terminus Clock. If you do so, until the end of that phase, subtract 1 from casting rolls for enemy **WIZARDS**.
6	**Standard of the Ulfenwatch:** *This now tattered banner was once the pride of the Ulfenkarn city guard. To look upon its twisted glory is to be reminded of the conquests of the Vyrkos.* Once per battle, at the start of the hero phase, you can say that the bearer will raise the standard of the Ulfenwatch. If you do so, until the end of that turn, each time your opponent spends a command point, roll a dice. On a 5+, you receive 1 extra command point.

KASTELAI DYNASTY

BATTLE TRAITS - THE SANGUINE LANCE

THE SHIFTING KEEP

None can predict where the Crimson Keep will manifest next, but wherever it appears, carnage will be total.

Instead of setting up a **Kastelai Dynasty Blood Knights** unit on the battlefield, you can place it to one side and say that it is set up in ambush as a reserve unit. You can set up 1 reserve unit in ambush for each unit you have already set up on the battlefield.

At the end of any of your movement phases, you can set up 1 or more of these units on the battlefield wholly within 6" of the battlefield edge and more than 9" from all enemy units. At the start of the fourth battle round, reserve units that are still in ambush are destroyed.

MIGHT OF THE CRIMSON KEEP

Kastelai vampires revel in displaying their martial skills, their fervour increasing as more foes fall before them.

Each time a friendly **Kastelai Dynasty Vampire** unit destroys an enemy unit, that friendly unit gains the relevant ability below for the rest of the battle. A unit cannot gain the same ability more than once per battle.

If the enemy unit was a **Hero** or **Monster**:

- ***Bloodied Strength:*** Add 1 to the Damage characteristic of melee weapons used by that unit (excluding mounts).

If the enemy unit had a Wounds characteristic of 3 or more and was not a **Hero** or **Monster**:

- ***Stolen Vitality:*** Add 1 to the Wounds characteristic of that unit.

If the enemy unit had a Wounds characteristic of 2 or less:

- ***Absorbed Speed:*** Add 2 to run and charge rolls for that unit.

COMMAND TRAITS - LORDS OF THE CRIMSON KEEP

Kastelai Dynasty general only.

D6	Command Trait
1	**Beacon of Bloodshed:** *This general hurls themselves at the foe until none are left standing.* After this general makes a charge move, you can pick 1 enemy unit within 1" of this general and roll a dice. On a 3+, that unit suffers D3 mortal wounds.
2	**Master of Retaliation:** *This general often leaves themselves exposed so they can strike back hard.* At the end of the combat phase, if any wounds or mortal wounds were allocated to this general in that phase and this general was not slain, you can pick 1 enemy unit within 1" of them and roll a dice. On a 2+, that unit suffers D3 mortal wounds.
3	**Power in the Blood:** *Even the scent of blood sees this general fight with redoubled fervour.* If an enemy unit is destroyed within 6" of this general, this general gains the relevant ability from the Might of the Crimson Keep battle trait above, even if the enemy unit was not destroyed by this general.
4	**Rousing Commander:** *When the time is right, this general sends their warriors into a frenzy.* Once per battle, at the start of the combat phase, you can say that this general will rouse their warriors. If you do so, until the end of that phase, friendly **Kastelai Dynasty Vampire** units wholly within 12" of this general benefit from the Bloodied Strength and Stolen Vitality abilities from the Might of the Crimson Keep battle trait above (if they have not already gained one or both of them).
5	**Swift and Deadly:** *Nothing delights this general more than seeing the Kastelai crash into the foe.* You can re-roll charge rolls for friendly **Kastelai Dynasty** units while they are wholly within 12" of this general.
6	**A Craving for Massacre:** *This general is forever straining with the need for bloodshed.* This general can run and still charge later in the same turn.

ARTEFACTS OF POWER - RELICS OF RED CONQUEST

KASTELAI DYNASTY HERO only.

D6	Artefact of Power
1	**Sword of the Red Seneschals:** *Status amongst the Kastelai is often marked by the wielding of grander weapons. This blood-forged longsword is a true masterwork and a worthy symbol for Vhordrai's chosen disciples.* Pick 1 of the bearer's melee weapons. In the combat phase, if any enemy models are slain by attacks made with that weapon, add 1 to wound rolls for attacks made by friendly **SOULBLIGHT GRAVELORDS** units wholly within 12" of the bearer until the end of that phase.
2	**Bloodsaint's Shield:** *Embedded in the draconic design upon this shield are shards of crushed nullstone that serve to deaden the aether around the bearer, leaving raw martial skill the only true measure of worth.* Subtract 1 from casting rolls for enemy **WIZARDS** within 6" of the bearer.
3	**Standard of the Crimson Keep:** *It is said that this darkly regal banner has been carried by many successive generations of vampiric knights and wards against those who would seek victory through dishonourable means.* Subtract 1 from hit rolls for attacks made with missile weapons that target the bearer.
4	**Grave-sand Shard:** *By crushing this vitrified gem of grave-sand between the fingers, a Kastelai vampire can draw upon a surge of death magic to reinvigorate their resurrected warriors.* Once per battle, at the start of the hero phase, you can say that the bearer will crush their grave-sand shard. If you do so, add 1 to rolls for the Deathless Minions battle trait (pg 73) for friendly **SOULBLIGHT GRAVELORDS** units wholly within 12" of the bearer until the end of that turn.
5	**Fragment of the Keep:** *Kastelai warriors dispatched on far-ranging errantry quests will often be gifted a single brick from the Crimson Keep, increasing their vitality tenfold.* Subtract 1 from wound rolls for attacks made with melee weapons by enemy units within 6" of the bearer.
6	**The Red Casket:** *Only the most battle-crazed vampire knights seek to be sealed into this cursed cuirass, as it transforms them into a whirlwind of mindless, frothing death.* Once per battle, at the start of your charge phase, you can say that the bearer will draw upon the power of the Red Casket. If you do so, add 3 to charge rolls for the bearer in that phase.

AVENGORII DYNASTY

BATTLE TRAITS - THE NIGHTMARE BROOD

CURSED ABOMINATIONS

The Avengorii Dynasty is known for taking to battle alongside a menagerie of necrotic horrors, some of which have become particularly infamous.

If a Soulblight Gravelords army with the **Avengorii Dynasty** keyword includes any **Terrorgheists** or **Zombie Dragons**, 1 of those models has a cursed mutation. Choose which model will have the cursed mutation, then pick from or roll on the Cursed Mutations table opposite.

You can choose 1 additional friendly **Avengorii Dynasty Terrorgheist** or **Avengorii Dynasty Zombie Dragon** to have a cursed mutation for each warscroll battalion in your army. A model cannot have more than 1 cursed mutation, and an army may not include duplicates of the same cursed mutation.

MONSTROUS MIGHT

So crazed and blood hungry are the monstrous lords of the Avengorii that only the most titanic blows can hope to faze them.

Subtract 1 from wound rolls for attacks made with melee weapons that target friendly **Avengorii Dynasty Terrorgheists**, **Avengorii Dynasty Zombie Dragons** or **Avengorii Dynasty Vampire Monsters** unless the attacking unit is a **Monster**.

UNSTOPPABLE NIGHTMARES

In succumbing to their bestial nature, the Avengorii have become true monsters that are nearly impossible to slay.

In the combat phase, you can pick 1 friendly **Avengorii Dynasty Terrorgheist**, **Avengorii Dynasty Zombie Dragon** or **Avengorii Dynasty Vampire Monster** to unleash its monstrous power. If you do so, until the end of that phase, use the top row on that model's damage table, regardless of how many wounds it has suffered. The same model cannot benefit from this ability more than once per battle.

COMMAND TRAITS - TWISTED PARAGONS

Avengorii Dynasty general only.

D3	Command Trait
1	**An Eye for An Eye:** *This general has retained their sanity better than some Avengorii, enough to lay cunning traps for unwary foes.* If any wounds or mortal wounds are allocated to this general in the combat phase, add 1 to the Damage characteristic of melee weapons used by this general (including their mount) until the end of that phase.
2	**Torment-driven Throes:** *Twisted limbs and tails lash out when this general fights, killing scores and debilitating those who remain.* At the start of the combat phase, you can roll a dice for each enemy unit within 3" of this general. On a 5+, that enemy unit suffers 1 mortal wound and can only attack this general in that phase after this general has already fought in that phase.
3	**Unhinged Rampager:** *This general's bestial hunger sees them close on the foe without hesitation.* You can re-roll charge rolls for this general.

ARTEFACTS OF POWER - MONSTROUS SPOILS

AVENGORII DYNASTY HERO only.

D3 Artefact of Power

1 Breath of the Void Maw: *These black shards, said to be crystallised motes of magic that escaped through the realmgate at the heart of the Avengorii's stronghold, can be shattered against the ground to summon a gale of killing Shyishan energies.*

Once per battle, in your hero phase, you can pick 1 enemy unit within 6" of the bearer that is visible to them and roll a dice. On a 3+, that unit suffers D6 mortal wounds.

2 Ghorvar's Collar: *The enchanted flesh-stitched ruff belonging to Ghorvar, the brutal former patriarch of the Avengorii, allowed him to cow any beast with but a glance. Such did not save him from the Mother of Nightmare's cold wrath, but his most famous relic remains a powerful tool of dominion.*

Once per battle, at the start of the combat phase, you can say that the bearer will don Ghorvar's collar. If you do so, you can re-roll wound rolls of 1 for attacks made by the bearer in that phase.

3 The Furious Crown: *Taken from a champion of Chaos slain on the orders of Lauka Vai, this crown seeks to dominate the wearer by inundating them with waves of fury. For the bestial Avengorii, however, this is little impediment to harnessing its power.*

Once per battle, at the start of your charge phase, you can say that the bearer will unleash the fury of the crown. If you do so, after the bearer makes a charge move in that phase, you can pick 1 enemy unit within 1" of the bearer and roll a number of dice equal to the charge roll for that charge move. For each 5+, that enemy unit suffers 1 mortal wound.

CURSED MUTATIONS

D3 Cursed Mutation

1 Maddening Hunger: *This monster does not care what it feasts upon, so long as the carnage is bloody and total.*

Once per turn, at the start of the combat phase, you can pick 1 enemy model with a Wounds characteristic of 1 that is within 3" of this model. If you do so, that enemy model is slain and you can heal 1 wound allocated to this model.

2 Urges of Atrocity: *This abomination sees no advantage in letting the fight come to it.*

Once per battle, this model can run and still charge later in the same turn.

3 Nullblood Construct: *So potent is the aura of ending-magic surrounding this beast that sorcery simply withers and dies in its presence.*

Re-roll successful casting rolls for enemy **WIZARDS** within 9" of this model.

SPELL LORES

Friendly **WIZARDS** in a Soulblight Gravelords army know the Invigorating Aura spell in addition to any other spells they know. Any number of **SOULBLIGHT GRAVELORDS WIZARDS** can attempt to cast Invigorating Aura in the same hero phase. In addition, you can choose or roll for 1 spell from one of the following tables for each **WIZARD** in a Soulblight Gravelords army. If **NAGASH** is part of a Soulblight Gravelords army, he knows all the spells in all of the following tables.

Invigorating Aura: *Invoking ancient necromantic rites, the caster bolsters their minions or returns them to cursed unlife.*

Invigorating Aura has a casting value of 8. Add 1 to the roll for each friendly **SOULBLIGHT GRAVELORDS HERO** on the battlefield. If successfully cast, pick 1 friendly **SOULBLIGHT GRAVELORDS SUMMONABLE** unit wholly within 18" of the caster. You can either heal up to 3 wounds allocated to that unit or, if no wounds are allocated to it, you can return a number of slain models to that unit that have a combined Wounds characteristic of 3 or less. The same unit cannot benefit from this spell more than once per turn.

LORE OF THE VAMPIRES

NAGASH and **VAMPIRE WIZARDS** only.

D6 Spell

1 Blades of Shyish: *The wizard summons a whirlwind of spirit-blades to slice through the foe.*

Blades of Shyish has a casting value of 5. If successfully cast, roll a dice for each enemy unit within 12" of the caster. On a 3+, that unit suffers 1 mortal wound.

2 Spirit Gale: *The wizard calls forth spectral winds that howl through the ranks of the enemy, tearing their souls from their bodies.*

Spirit Gale has a casting value of 5. If successfully cast, pick 1 enemy unit within 18" of the caster that is visible to them and roll 2D6. If the roll is greater than that unit's Bravery characteristic, that unit suffers a number of mortal wounds equal to the difference between its Bravery characteristic and the roll.

3 Soulpike: *The caster places a hex on the foe so that, should they move too aggressively, they risk impaling their own souls on a shimmering forest of purple-black spears.*

Soulpike has a casting value of 6. If successfully cast, pick 1 enemy unit within 18" of the caster that is visible to them. Until your next hero phase, if that unit makes a charge move, roll a number of dice equal to the charge roll for that unit. For each 4+, that unit suffers 1 mortal wound. The same unit cannot be affected by this spell more than once per turn.

4 Amethystine Pinions: *Incorporeal amethyst wings grow from the caster's back, allowing them to race across the battlefield.*

Amethystine Pinions has a casting value of 5. If successfully cast, until your next hero phase, add 6" to the caster's Move characteristic. The same unit cannot benefit from this spell more than once per turn.

5 Vile Transference: *The caster siphons the animus from nearby foes and uses it to rejuvenate their ageless form.*

Vile Transference has a casting value of 4. If successfully cast, pick 1 enemy unit within 6" of the caster that is visible to them. Roll a number of dice equal to half of that enemy unit's Wounds characteristic (rounding up). For each 6, you can heal 1 wound allocated to the caster.

6 Amaranthine Orb: *The wizard hurls a pulsing globe of pure necrotic magic that turns flesh and bone to ash in an instant.*

Amaranthine Orb has a casting value of 6. If successfully cast, pick 1 point on the battlefield within 9" of the caster that is visible to them and draw an imaginary straight line 1mm wide between that point and the closest part of the caster's base. Roll a dice for each unit that has models passed across by this line. On a 2+, that unit suffers D3 mortal wounds. **DEATH** units are not affected by this spell.

LORE OF THE DEATHMAGES

NAGASH, MORTARCHS and DEATHMAGES WIZARDS only.

D6 Spell

1 Overwhelming Dread: *The target of this curse is overcome with a sensation of creeping doom, causing them to cower in fear.*

Overwhelming Dread has a casting value of 5. If successfully cast, pick 1 enemy unit within 18" of the caster that is visible to them. Until your next hero phase, subtract 1 from hit rolls for attacks made by that unit.

2 Fading Vigour: *The wizard saps the vitality from their enemies until they can barely raise their weapons.*

Fading Vigour has a casting value of 6. If successfully cast, pick 1 enemy unit within 18" of the caster that is visible to them. Subtract 1 from the Attacks characteristic of that unit's melee weapons (to a minimum of 1) until your next hero phase.

3 Spectral Grasp: *With a gesture, the caster summons dozens of spectral hands into existence that grasp hold of nearby enemies.*

Spectral Grasp has a casting value of 6. If successfully cast, pick 1 terrain feature wholly within 18" of the caster that is visible to them. Until your next hero phase, halve the Move characteristic (rounding down) of enemy units that start a normal move within 3" of that terrain feature.

4 Prison of Grief: *The caster curses his victims to relive the greatest tragedy in their lives, drowning their will to fight in waves of sorrow and self-pity.*

Prison of Grief has a casting value of 6. If successfully cast, pick 1 enemy unit within 12" of the caster that is visible to them. Until your next hero phase, roll a dice each time that unit attempts to move. On a 5+, that unit cannot move in that phase. The same unit cannot be affected by this spell more than once per turn.

5 Decrepify: *The wizard causes the muscles of an enemy champion to atrophy, robbing them of their strength.*

Decrepify has a casting value of 6. If successfully cast, pick 1 enemy **HERO** within 18" of the caster that is visible to them. Until your next hero phase, subtract 1 from wound rolls for attacks made by that model and subtract 1 from the Damage characteristic of that model's melee weapons (to a minimum of 1).

6 Soul Harvest: *The caster summons a ghostly scythe that slices through their enemies, cutting the cord tethering spirit to flesh.*

Soul Harvest has a casting value of 7. If successfully cast, each enemy unit within 3" of the caster suffers D3 mortal wounds. In addition, for each mortal wound inflicted by this spell and not negated, roll a dice. For each 5+, you can heal 1 wound allocated to the caster.

BATTLEPLAN

THE BELL TOLLS FOR THEE

Death is relentless, inevitable and inescapable. So too, therefore, are the forces of the Soulblight Gravelords. When the vampires march to war, they turn horror and atrocity themselves into weapons. Perhaps, in some ways, theirs is a worse crime even than that of the champions of Chaos. Unlike those ruinous warriors, the undead do not butcher and terrorise to serve parasitic gods; they do so purely to prove their mastery over the living and to satiate their vile cravings. A Soulblight warlord will think nothing of massacring entire townships or cities simply to add new unliving warriors to their armies, hurling those swollen hordes at the enemy in a tide of shambling flesh and clattering bone.

This battleplan lets you recreate just such a full-scale assault with your Soulblight Gravelords army. The vampires have raised a truly vast host and are now sending it to crush the last bastion of living defence in this region. Their minds bleached by horror, the defenders know that failure here will mean the demise of all that they value. How long will they last against the endless legions of shambling revenants?

THE ARMIES

Each player picks an army. One player is the Soulblight Gravelords player. Their opponent is the Dauntless Defender. The Soulblight Gravelords player must use a Soulblight Gravelords army.

THE BATTLEFIELD

First, place 3 markers in the locations shown on the map to represent gravesites for the purposes of the Unquiet Dead battle trait. Do not pick any other points to be gravesites for this battle.

SET-UP

The Soulblight Gravelords player sets up their army first, wholly within their territory. The Dauntless Defender then sets up their army wholly within their territory. The territories are shown on the map.

FIRST TURN

The Soulblight Gravelords player takes the first turn in the first battle round.

COMMAND ABILITY

The following additional command ability can be used in this battle.

Cut Them Down!: *Defeat here would mean the subjugation of all life in this region. The warriors standing against the deathly droves simply cannot fail, and at the inspirational beckoning of their commanders, they will dig deep to unleash deadly attacks.*

The Dauntless Defender can use this command ability at the start of the combat phase. If they do so, they can pick 1 friendly unit wholly within 12" of a friendly **HERO**. Add 1 to the Damage characteristic of melee weapons used by that unit until the start of their next hero phase. A unit cannot benefit from this command ability more than once per phase.

DEFIANT TO THE LAST

The living have nowhere left to run, and so broken are their minds with terror that they refuse to abandon their posts for as long as they draw breath.

Do not take battleshock tests for units in the Dauntless Defender's army.

ETERNAL HORDES

Such is the power of the Gravelords' re-animating sorcery that their minions can be cut down in one instant and set upon another victim in the next.

At the end of each turn, the Soulblight Gravelords player can pick 1 friendly **SOULBLIGHT GRAVELORDS SUMMONABLE** unit that is wholly within 12" of a friendly **SOULBLIGHT GRAVELORDS HERO** and roll a dice for each model in that unit that was slain in that turn. On a 5+, they can return that slain model to that unit. Set up the returning models one at a time within 1" of a model from the unit they are returning to (this can be a model returned earlier in the phase). Returning models can only be set up within 3" of an enemy unit if any models from the unit they are returning to are already within 3" of that enemy unit.

BATTLE LENGTH

Starting from the fourth battle round, at the end of each battle round, roll a dice and add the number of the current battle round to the roll. On a 9+, the battle ends. On any other roll, the battle continues.

GLORIOUS VICTORY

The Soulblight Gravelords player wins a **major victory** if more than half of the units in the Dauntless Defender's starting army have been destroyed when the battle ends.

The Dauntless Defender wins a **major victory** if more than half of the units in their starting army have not been destroyed when the battle ends.

If neither player has won a **major victory** when the battle ends, each player must add up the Wounds characteristics of all enemy **HEROES** slain during the battle. The player with the higher total wins a **minor victory**. Any other result is a **draw**.

PATH TO GLORY

Path to Glory campaigns centre around collecting and fighting a series of battles in the Mortal Realms. Players start off with a small warband. Over the course of several battles, each warband will gather more followers to join them in their quest for glory and renown.

In order to take part in a Path to Glory campaign, you will need two or more players. Each player will need a **Hero** to be their champion and must then create a warband to follow and fight beside their champion during the campaign.

The players fight battles against each other using the warbands they have created. The results of these battles will gain their warbands glory. After battle, warbands may swell in numbers as more warriors flock to their banner, or existing troops may become more powerful.

After gaining sufficient glory or growing your warband enough to dominate all others through sheer weight of numbers, you will be granted a final test. Succeed, and you will be crowned the victor of the campaign, your glory affirmed for all time.

CREATING A WARBAND

In a Path to Glory game, you do not select your army in the normal manner. Instead, you create a warband that consists of a mighty champion, battling to earn the favour of the gods, and their followers. The details and progress of each warband need to be recorded on a warband roster, which you can download for free from games-workshop.com.

To create a warband, simply follow these steps and record the results on your warband roster:

1. First, pick a faction for your warband. Each faction has its own set of warband tables that are used to generate the units in the warband and the rewards they can receive for fighting battles. The warband tables included in this battletome let you collect a Soulblight Gravelords warband, but other Warhammer Age of Sigmar publications include warband tables to let you collect warbands from other factions.

2. Next, choose your warband's champion by selecting one of the options from your faction's champion table. Give your champion a suitably grand name and write this down on your warband roster.

3. Having picked your champion, the next step is to make follower rolls to generate your starting followers. The champion you chose in step 2 will determine how many follower rolls you have. To make a follower roll, pick a column from one of the followers tables and then roll a dice. If you prefer, instead of rolling a dice, you can pick the result from the followers table (this still uses up the roll).

   Sometimes a table will require you to expend two or more rolls, or one roll and a number of Glory Points (see Gaining Glory), in order to use it. Note that the option to expend Glory Points can only be used when you add new followers to your warband after a battle (see Rewards of Battle). In either case, in order to generate a follower unit from the table, you must have enough rolls and/or Glory Points to meet the requirements, and you can then either roll once on the table or pick one result from the table of your choice. If you expend Glory Points, you must reduce your Glory Points total by the amount shown on the table.

   Followers are organised into units. The followers table tells you how many models the unit has. Follower units cannot include additional models, but they can otherwise take any options listed on their warscroll. Record all of the information about your followers on your warband roster.

4. You can use 1 follower roll to allow your champion to start the campaign with a Champion's Reward or to allow 1 of your follower units to start the campaign with a Follower's Reward (see Rewards of Battle).

5. Finally, give your warband a name, one that will inspire respect and dread in your rivals. Your warband is now complete and you can fight your first battle. Good luck!

TO WAR!

Having created a warband, you can now fight battles with it against other warbands taking part in the campaign. You can fight battles as and when you wish, and you can use any of the battleplans available for Warhammer Age of Sigmar. The units you use for a game must be those on your roster.

When you use a Soulblight Gravelords warband in a Path to Glory game, you can use all the battle traits from page 73. You cannot use the Cursed Bloodlines battle trait or any other Soulblight Gravelords allegiance abilities.

Any casualties suffered by a warband are assumed to have been replaced in time for its next battle. If your champion is slain in a battle, it is assumed that they were merely injured; they are back to full strength for your next game, thirsty for vengeance!

GAINING GLORY

All of the players in the campaign are vying for glory. The amount of glory they have received is represented by the Glory Points that the warband has accumulated.

As a warband's glory increases, it will also attract additional followers, and a warband's champion may be granted rewards.

Warbands receive Glory Points after a battle is complete. If the warband drew or lost the battle, it receives 1 Glory Point. If it won the battle, it receives D3 Glory Points (re-roll a result of 1 if it won a **major victory**).

Add the Glory Points you scored to the total recorded on your roster. Once you have won 10 Glory Points, you will have a chance to win the campaign (see Eternal Glory).

REWARDS OF BATTLE

After each battle, you can take one of the three following options. Alternatively, roll a D3 to determine which option to take.

D3	Option
1	**Additional Followers:** *More loyal followers flock to your banner.* You receive 1 follower roll that can be used to select a new unit from a followers table and add it to your warband roster. See step 3 of Creating a Warband for details of how to use the followers table to add a unit to your warband. Once 5 new units have joined your warband, you will have a chance to win the campaign (see Eternal Glory).
2	**Champion's Reward:** *Your champion's prowess grows.* Roll on the champion rewards table for your warband and note the result on your warband roster. Your champion can only receive 1 Champion's Reward – if they already have a Champion's Reward, you must take a Follower's Reward instead.
3	**Follower's Reward:** *Your warriors become renowned for mighty deeds.* Pick 1 unit of followers and then roll on the followers rewards table for your warband. Note the result on your warband roster. A unit can only receive 1 Follower's Reward. If all of your follower units have a Follower's Reward, you must take Additional Followers instead.

ETERNAL GLORY

There are two ways to win a Path to Glory campaign: by Blood or by Might. To win by Blood, your warband must first have 10 Glory Points. To win by Might, your warband must have at least 5 additional units of followers. In either case, you must then fight and win one more battle to win the campaign. If the next battle you fight is tied or lost, you do not receive any Glory Points – just keep on fighting battles until you win the campaign… or another player wins first!

You can shorten or lengthen a campaign by lowering or raising the number of Glory Points needed to win by Blood or the number of extra units that must join a warband to win by Might. For example, for a shorter campaign, you could say that a warband only needs 5 Glory Points before the final fight, or for a longer one, you could say that 15 are needed.

SOULBLIGHT GRAVELORDS WARBAND TABLES

Use the following tables to determine the champion that leads your warband, the followers that make up the units that fight at their side, and the rewards they receive after battle.

CHAMPION TABLE

Champion	Follower Rolls
Vampire Lord on Zombie Dragon	3
Bloodseeker Palanquin	4
Coven Throne	4
Vengorian Lord	4
Necromancer	6
Vampire Lord	6
Wight King or Wight King on Skeletal Steed	6

RETINUE FOLLOWERS TABLE

D6	Followers
1	20 Deadwalker Zombies
2	10 Dire Wolves
3	10 Deathrattle Skeletons
4	5 Grave Guard
5	5 Black Knights
6	3 Fell Bats

HERO FOLLOWERS TABLE

D3	Followers
1	1 Wight King
2	1 Necromancer
3	1 Vampire Lord

ELITE RETINUE FOLLOWERS TABLE
(uses 2 rolls, or 1 roll and 1 Glory Point)

D3	Followers
1	1 Corpse Cart with Unholy Lodestone or 1 Corpse Cart with Balefire Brazier
2	3 Vargheists
3	5 Blood Knights

BEHEMOTH RETINUE FOLLOWERS TABLE
(uses 3 rolls, or 1 roll and 2 Glory Points)

D3	Followers
1	1 Mortis Engine
2	1 Terrorgheist
3	1 Zombie Dragon

CHAMPION REWARDS TABLE

2D6 Reward

2 Immortal Majesty: *When this champion marches out to accomplish their designs, they do so in such macabre splendour that the living cannot help but quail before them.*

If an enemy unit fails a battleshock test within 3" of this champion, add D3 to the number of models that flee.

3 Favoured Retainers: *Deathrattle legions are favoured tools of this champion, and they enact their master's plots with unfeeling dedication.*

Ignore negative modifiers to hit and wound rolls for attacks made with melee weapons by friendly DEATHRATTLE units while they are wholly within 12" of this champion.

4 Swift Form: *Whether transforming into a bestial creature or dissipating into dark mist, this champion can cover ground with terrible swiftness.*

Add 2 to run and charge rolls for this champion.

5 Premeditated Violence: *This champion has extensively taken the measure of their foes and knows just where to strike for maximum effect.*

If the unmodified hit roll for an attack made with a melee weapon by this champion is 6, that attack scores 2 hits on the target instead of 1. Make a wound and save roll for each hit.

6 Aura of Dark Majesty: *The beguiling aura that swathes this champion can leave an enemy's blade slack and aimless in their grip.*

Subtract 1 from hit rolls for attacks made with melee weapons that target this champion.

7 Unholy Impetus: *As this champion indulges their bloodthirst, the souls of the freshly slain are used to empower the undead hordes.*

In the combat phase, if any enemy models are slain by attacks made with melee weapons by this champion in that phase, add 1 to the Attacks characteristic of melee weapons used by friendly units wholly within 12" of this champion until the end of that phase.

8 Master of Retaliation: *This champion often leaves themselves exposed so they can strike back hard.*

At the end of the combat phase, if any wounds or mortal wounds were allocated to this champion in that phase and this champion was not slain, you can pick 1 enemy unit within 1" of them and roll a dice. On a 2+, that unit suffers D3 mortal wounds.

9 A Craving for Massacre: *This champion is a red-handed butcher, forever straining with the need for bloodshed.*

This champion can run and still charge later in the same turn.

10 Kin of the Wolf: *Letting out a lupine howl, this champion summons packs of undead wolves to the field.*

Once per battle, at the end of your movement phase, you can say that this champion will summon a pack of Dire Wolves to the battlefield. If you do so, you can add 1 unit of up to 5 DIRE WOLVES to your army. Set up that unit wholly within 9" of this champion and more than 9" from all enemy units.

11 Spoor Trackers: *So potent is this champion's bestial soul that even the shambling undead act with increased haste in their presence.*

At the start of your hero phase, friendly units wholly within 9" of this champion can make a normal move of up to 3" (they cannot run).

12 An Eye for An Eye: *This champion has retained their sanity better than some Avengorii, enough to lay cunning traps for unwary foes.*

If any wounds or mortal wounds are allocated to this champion in the combat phase, add 1 to the Damage characteristic of melee weapons used by this champion (including their mount) until the end of that phase.

HERO, RETINUE AND ELITE RETINUE FOLLOWERS REWARDS TABLE

D6	Reward
1	**The Bait:** *These silent revenants are expected to draw the wrath of the enemy onto them, enduring long enough for the vampires to strike.* Add 1 to save rolls for attacks that target this unit while it is wholly within your territory.
2	**Ageless Cunning:** *Upon scenting weakness, these warriors will strike from an unexpected angle, emerging from a pall of midnight to lay waste to their unprepared foes.* Instead of setting up this unit on the battlefield, you can place it to one side and say that it is set up in ambush as a reserve unit. At the end of any of your movement phases, you can set up this unit on the battlefield, wholly within 6" of the edge of the battlefield and more than 9" from any enemy units.
3	**Merciless Hunters:** *The only victory for these warriors is the complete obliteration of their foe.* Add 1 to wound rolls for attacks made with melee weapons by this unit.
4	**Terrifying Visage:** *The foes of these warriors are stricken with dread merely upon looking at them.* Subtract 1 from wound rolls for attacks made with melee weapons that target this unit.
5	**Swift and Deadly:** *Nothing delights these warriors more than crashing into a reeling foe.* You can re-roll charge rolls for this unit.
6	**Torment-driven Throes:** *Twisted limbs and tails lash out when these warriors fight, killing scores and debilitating those who remain.* At the start of the combat phase, you can roll a dice for each enemy unit within 3" of this unit. On a 5+, that enemy unit suffers 1 mortal wound and can only attack this unit in that phase after this unit has already fought in that phase.

BEHEMOTH RETINUE FOLLOWERS REWARDS TABLE

D3	Reward
1	**Monstrous Might:** *So crazed and blood hungry is this menace that only the most titanic blows can hope to faze it.* Subtract 1 from wound rolls for attacks made with melee weapons that target this unit.
2	**Accursed Regeneration:** *Endless foul regeneration is but one of the many 'gifts' that this cursed menace possesses.* In your hero phase, you can heal up to D3 wounds allocated to this unit.
3	**Unstoppable Nightmare:** *This behemoth has become a true monster that is nearly impossible to slay.* Once per battle, in the combat phase, you can say that this unit will unleash its monstrous power. If you do so, until the end of that phase, use the top row on that unit's damage table, regardless of how many wounds it has suffered.

WARSCROLLS

WARSCROLL BATTALION

LEGION OF SHYISH

A Legion of Shyish is a nightmare given form, a seemingly endless horde of the risen dead driven against the bastions of the living. Such is the concentration of necromantic power drawn to these hosts that undead warriors rise again almost as soon as they are struck down, hacking down the foe through relentless attrition.

ORGANISATION

- 1 Red Banqueters
- 1 Deathmarch
- 1 Fellwing Flock
- 1 Deathstench Drove

ABILITIES

Horror Unending: *The never-ending waves of deathly minions summoned by the Legion of Shyish shatter all hopes of victory for those who stand against them.*

Do not roll a dice to determine the number of wounds healed or models returned by the Deathly Invocation battle trait for a friendly SOULBLIGHT GRAVELORDS SUMMONABLE unit in this battalion. Instead, you can heal up to 3 wounds allocated to that unit or, if no wounds are allocated to it, you can return a number of slain models to that unit that have a combined Wounds characteristic of 3 or less.

This section includes Soulblight Gravelords warscrolls and warscroll battalions. Updated May 2021; the warscrolls printed here take precedence over any warscrolls with an earlier publication date or no publication date.

WARSCROLL BATTALION

RED BANQUETERS

To the vampires, the battlefield is a feasting hall where they can satiate their most gory cravings. Courts of these unliving nobles will sometimes band together – all the better to eviscerate their enemies.

ORGANISATION

- 2+ Vampire Lords
- 1 Bloodseeker Palanquin or 1 Coven Throne
- 2+ Blood Knights units

ABILITIES

The Blood is the Life: *Those who bear the Soulblight curse constantly crave fresh gore. When many such creatures gather, their bloodthirsty excesses are horrific to behold.*

In your hero phase, you can heal up to D3 wounds allocated to each unit in this battalion.

WARSCROLL BATTALION

FELLWING FLOCK

Fellwing Flocks are packs of aerial predators marked by the Soulblight curse. These creatures dive upon the foe without pause or warning, taking a bestial satisfaction in the slaughter that follows.

ORGANISATION

- 2-3 Vargheists units
- 2-3 Fell Bats units

ABILITIES

Swooping Predators: *These vicious winged monstrosities soar over the shambling horde, diving down and tearing apart their prey with a merciless fury.*

Add 1 to hit rolls for attacks made with melee weapons by units in this battalion if those units made a charge move in the same turn.

WARSCROLL BATTALION

DEATHSTENCH DROVE

Moaning mindlessly, the Deadwalkers of a Deathstench Drove shamble towards the foe with unstoppable determination, reinforced by the arcane Corpse Carts that rattle alongside them.

ORGANISATION

- 1-2 **Corpse Carts**
- 2 Dire Wolves units
- 2 Deadwalker Zombies units

ABILITIES

Nexus of Malevolence: *The Corpse Carts that rattle alongside Deathstench Droves are driven by the most ancient and accomplished Corpsemasters and are potent loci of deathly magic.*

Add 1 to the Attacks characteristic of melee weapons used by units in this battalion while those units are wholly within 12" of any **Corpse Carts** in this battalion.

WARSCROLL BATTALION

DEATHMARCH

The barrow legions of the Deathrattle attack with a relentless focus, directed onwards by their Wight King masters and assailing the foe in a tide of rusted blades.

ORGANISATION

- 1 **Wight King**
- 1-3 Black Knights units
- 1-3 Grave Guard units
- 2+ Deathrattle Skeletons units

ABILITIES

March of the Dead: *A Wight King's sheer force of will and rasped commands sees his Deathrattle minions advance with great surety and focus.*

At the start of your movement phase, you can pick up to 3 different friendly units in this battalion that are wholly within 12" of this battalion's **Wight King**. If you do so, add 3" to the Move characteristic of each of those units in that phase (they can still either run or charge).

• WARSCROLL •

NAGASH

SUPREME LORD OF THE UNDEAD

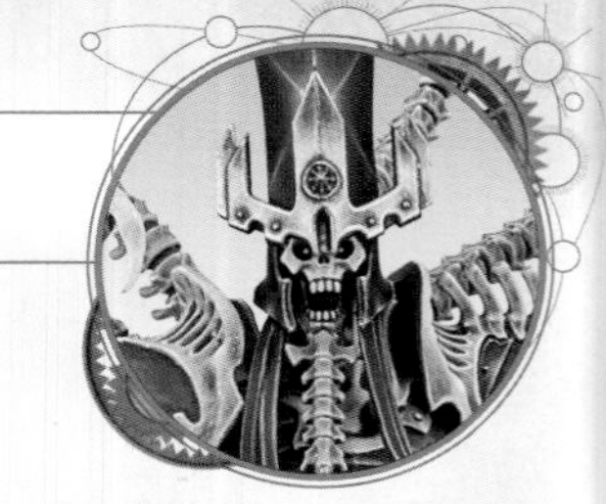

Nagash is the God of Death, hateful and ancient beyond mortal reckoning. When the Great Necromancer takes to the battlefield, the earth writhes as scores of undead warriors crawl forth from the grave to serve their eternal master.

MISSILE WEAPONS	Range	Attacks	To Hit	To Wound	Rend	Damage
Gaze of Nagash	12"	1	3+	2+	-1	D6
MELEE WEAPONS	**Range**	**Attacks**	**To Hit**	**To Wound**	**Rend**	**Damage**
Alakanash	3"	1	3+	2+	-3	D6
Zefet-nebtar	2"	✹	3+	3+	-2	3
Spectral Claws and Daggers	1"	6	5+	4+	-	1

DAMAGE TABLE			
Wounds Suffered	**The Nine Books of Nagash**	**Zefet-nebtar**	**Staff of Power**
0-3	Cast and unbind 5 extra spells	6	+3 cast /+3 unbind or dispel
4-6	Cast and unbind 4 extra spells	5	+3 cast /+2 unbind or dispel
7-10	Cast and unbind 3 extra spells	4	+2 cast /+2 unbind or dispel
11-13	Cast and unbind 2 extra spells	3	+2 cast /+1 unbind or dispel
14+	Cast and unbind 1 extra spells	2	+1 cast /+1 unbind or dispel

DESCRIPTION

Nagash is a named character that is a single model. He is armed with Zefet-nebtar, Alakanash and the Gaze of Nagash.

COMPANION: Nagash is accompanied by a host of spirits that fight with their Spectral Claws and Daggers. For rules purposes, they are treated in the same manner as a mount.

FLY: Nagash can fly.

ABILITIES

Alakanash, the Staff of Power: *This staff is capped with gems of purest Shyishan realmstone.*

Add the Staff of Power value shown on this model's damage table to casting, dispelling and unbinding rolls for this model. In addition, this model can attempt to cast Arcane Bolt and Mystic Shield any number of times in the same hero phase, even if another **WIZARD** has already attempted to cast the spell in that phase.

Invocation of Nagash: *With but a thought, Nagash can call forth fresh minions to assail his foes.*

At the start of your hero phase, if this model is on the battlefield, you can pick up to 5 different friendly **SUMMONABLE** units or friendly **OSSIARCH BONEREAPERS** units in any combination. For each of those units, you can either heal up to 3 wounds that have been allocated to that unit or, if no wounds have been allocated to it, you can return a number of slain models to that unit with a combined Wounds characteristic of 3 or less.

Frightful Touch: *The malign spirits that surround Nagash can freeze an opponent's blood with a single touch.*

If the unmodified hit roll for an attack made with this model's Spectral Claws and Daggers is 6, that attack inflicts 1 mortal wound on the target and the attack sequence ends (do not make a wound or save roll).

Morikhane: *This ensorcelled armour protects Nagash from arcane as well as physical attacks and can even cause an intense magical backlash on those that dare strike him.*

Roll a dice each time you allocate a mortal wound to this model. On a 1-3, nothing happens. On a 4-5, that mortal wound is negated. On a 6, that mortal wound is negated and the attacking unit suffers 1 mortal wound.

The Nine Books of Nagash: *Over his impossibly long existence, Nagash has collected a vast library of esoteric lore.*

The Nine Books of Nagash allow Nagash to cast extra spells in your hero phase and unbind extra spells in the enemy hero phase. The number of extra spells he can attempt to cast or unbind is shown on this model's damage table.

MAGIC

Nagash is a **WIZARD**. He can attempt to cast 3 spells in your hero phase and attempt to unbind 3 spells in the enemy hero phase (he can also attempt to cast and unbind extra spells due to the Nine Books of Nagash ability). He knows the Arcane Bolt, Mystic Shield, Hand of Dust and Soul Stealer spells.

Hand of Dust: *It is said that the touch of Nagash can wither and age any mortal, turning them to little more than a pile of dusty bones in mere moments.*

Hand of Dust has a casting value of 8. If successfully cast, pick 1 enemy model within 3" of the caster. Then, take a dice and hide it in one of your hands. Your opponent must pick one of your hands. If they pick the one holding the dice, the spell has no effect. If they pick the empty hand, the enemy model is slain.

Soul Stealer: *Nagash can siphon souls from the living to heal his own wounds.*

Soul Stealer has a casting value of 6. If successfully cast, pick 1 enemy unit within 24" of the caster that is visible to them and roll 2D6. If the roll is greater than that unit's Bravery characteristic, it suffers D3 mortal wounds. If the roll is at least double that unit's Bravery characteristic, it suffers D6 mortal wounds instead. You can heal up to 1 wound that has been allocated to the caster for each mortal wound inflicted by this spell that is not negated.

COMMAND ABILITIES

Supreme Lord of the Undead: *Nagash is the undisputed master of all undead creatures.*

You can use this command ability in your hero phase if this model is on the battlefield. If you do so, until your next hero phase, you can re-roll hit rolls of 1 for attacks made by friendly **DEATH** units, you can re-roll save rolls of 1 for attacks that target friendly **DEATH** units, and do not take battleshock tests for friendly **DEATH** units.

KEYWORDS	DEATH, DEATHLORDS, MONSTER, HERO, WIZARD, NAGASH

• WARSCROLL •

MANNFRED VON CARSTEIN

MORTARCH OF NIGHT

Few creatures are as embittered, or as cunning, as Mannfred von Carstein. There is no stratagem he will not employ, from unceremoniously dragging down the foe beneath hordes of zombies to using their very souls to power his fell magics.

MELEE WEAPONS	Range	Attacks	To Hit	To Wound	Rend	Damage
Gheistvor	1"	4	3+	3+	-1	D3
Sickle-glaive	2"	2	3+	3+	-1	2
Ebon Claws	1"	✸	4+	3+	-2	2
Spectral Claws and Daggers	1"	6	5+	4+	-	1

DAMAGE TABLE		
Wounds Suffered	Move	Ebon Claws
0-2	16"	6
3-4	13"	5
5-6	10"	4
7-8	7"	3
9+	4"	2

DESCRIPTION

Mannfred von Carstein is a named character that is a single model. He is armed with Gheistvor and a Sickle-glaive.

If this model is included in a Soulblight Gravelords army with the LEGION OF NIGHT lineage keyword, this model is treated as a general in addition to the model that is chosen to be the army general.

MOUNT: Mannfred von Carstein's dread abyssal, Ashigaroth, attacks with its Ebon Claws.

COMPANION: Mannfred von Carstein is accompanied by a host of spirits that attack with their Spectral Claws and Daggers. For rules purposes, they are treated in the same manner as a mount.

FLY: Mannfred von Carstein can fly.

ABILITIES

The Hunger: *Soulblight creatures crave the taste of blood and are empowered when they drink deep from the veins of defeated foes.*

At the end of the combat phase, if any enemy models were slain by wounds inflicted by this model's attacks in that phase, you can heal up to D3 wounds allocated to this model.

Armour of Templehof: *This suit of gothic armour is laden with many a fell enchantment, designed to protect its paranoid bearer from harm.*

The first wound or mortal wound allocated to this model in each phase is negated.

Sword of Unholy Power: *This unholy blade drinks deep of its victim's souls, bolstering Mannfred's power and that of his risen minions.*

If any enemy models are slain by wounds inflicted by this model's Gheistvor, until the end of that phase, add 1 to the Attacks characteristic of melee weapons used by friendly SOULBLIGHT GRAVELORDS SUMMONABLE units while they are wholly within 12" of this model.

Mortarch of Night: *Mannfred's cunning and tactical nous is legendary, his ability to exploit even the briefest of opportunities rightly infamous throughout the realms.*

At the start of the combat phase, if this model is within 3" of any enemy units, you can remove this model from the battlefield and set it up again anywhere on the battlefield more than 9" from all enemy units.

Frightful Touch: *The malign spirits that surround Mannfred can freeze an opponent's blood with a single touch.*

If the unmodified hit roll for an attack made with this model's Spectral Claws and Daggers is 6, that attack inflicts 1 mortal wound on the target and the attack sequence ends (do not make a wound or save roll).

MAGIC

Mannfred von Carstein is a WIZARD. He can attempt to cast 2 spells in your hero phase and attempt to unbind 2 spells in the enemy hero phase. He knows the Arcane Bolt, Mystic Shield and Wind of Death spells.

Wind of Death: *Mannfred conjures a gust of spectral wind that tears the souls from the bodies of any who feel its chilling bite.*

Wind of Death has a casting value of 7. If successfully cast, pick 1 enemy unit within 18" of the caster that is visible to them, and roll a dice for that enemy unit and each other enemy unit within 6" of that enemy unit. On a 3+, that unit suffers D3 mortal wounds.

COMMAND ABILITIES

Vigour of Undeath: *Lifting the Sword of Unholy Power high, Mannfred flexes his will and sends his servants forth with redoubled fervour.*

You can use this command ability once per turn in your hero phase. If you do so, add 1 to hit and wound rolls for friendly SOULBLIGHT GRAVELORDS units wholly within 12" of this model until your next hero phase.

KEYWORDS	DEATH, VAMPIRE, SOULBLIGHT GRAVELORDS, DEATHLORDS, LEGION OF NIGHT, MONSTER, HERO, WIZARD, MORTARCH, MANNFRED

• WARSCROLL •

NEFERATA

MORTARCH OF BLOOD

First amongst the Soulblight vampires, Neferata is a true monarch of the dead. In battle, the Nulahmian queen fights with a cruel, merciless intensity, the enemy's greatest warriors torn apart by a blur of precise and deadly strikes.

MELEE WEAPONS	Range	Attacks	To Hit	To Wound	Rend	Damage
Akmet-har	1"	5	2+	3+	-1	1
Aken-seth	1"	2	2+	3+	-2	2
Abyssal Talons	1"	✹	4+	3+	-2	2
Spectral Claws and Daggers	1"	6	5+	4+	-	1

DAMAGE TABLE		
Wounds Suffered	Move	Abyssal Talons
0-2	16"	6
3-4	13"	5
5-6	10"	4
7-8	7"	3
9+	4"	2

DESCRIPTION

Neferata is a named character that is a single model. She is armed with Akmet-har and Aken-seth.

If this model is included in a Soulblight Gravelords army with the LEGION OF BLOOD lineage keyword, this model is treated as a general in addition to the model that is chosen to be the army general.

MOUNT: Neferata's dread abyssal, Nagadron, attacks with its Abyssal Talons.

COMPANION: Neferata is accompanied by a host of spirits that attack with their Spectral Claws and Daggers. For rules purposes, they are treated in the same manner as a mount.

FLY: Neferata can fly.

ABILITIES

Dagger of Jet: *The dagger Akmet-har has been employed in many of Nulahmia's most sordid blood rituals and is capable of killing with the merest scratch.*

At the end of any phase, if any wounds inflicted by this model's Akmet-har in that phase were allocated to an enemy HERO and not negated, and that enemy model has not been slain, roll a dice. On a 5+, that enemy HERO is slain.

Mortarch of Blood: *An ancient and powerful vampire, Neferata sustains herself with the fresh blood of choice victims.*

At the end of the combat phase, if any enemy models were slain by wounds inflicted by this model's attacks in that phase, you can heal up to D6 wounds allocated to this model.

Frightful Touch: *The malign spirits that surround Neferata can freeze an opponent's blood with a single touch.*

If the unmodified hit roll for an attack made with this model's Spectral Claws and Daggers is 6, that attack inflicts 1 mortal wound on the target and the attack sequence ends (do not make a wound or save roll).

MAGIC

Neferata is a WIZARD. She can attempt to cast 2 spells in your hero phase and attempt to unbind 2 spells in the enemy hero phase. She knows the Arcane Bolt, Mystic Shield and Dark Mist spells.

Dark Mist: *At Neferata's arcane command, tendrils of dark mist coil around her minions, rendering their corporeal forms as insubstantial as smoke.*

Dark Mist has a casting value of 6. If successfully cast, pick 1 friendly SOULBLIGHT GRAVELORDS unit wholly within 12" of the caster. Ignore negative modifiers when making save rolls for attacks that target that unit until your next hero phase.

COMMAND ABILITIES

Twilight's Allure: *Neferata cloaks her minions in a penumbral gloom, shrouding the progress of her insidious schemes until it is too late to halt them.*

You can use this command ability once per turn in your hero phase. If you do so, subtract 1 from hit rolls for attacks made with melee weapons that target friendly SOULBLIGHT GRAVELORDS units wholly within 12" of this model until your next hero phase.

KEYWORDS	DEATH, VAMPIRE, SOULBLIGHT GRAVELORDS, DEATHLORDS, LEGION OF BLOOD, MONSTER, HERO, WIZARD, MORTARCH, NEFERATA

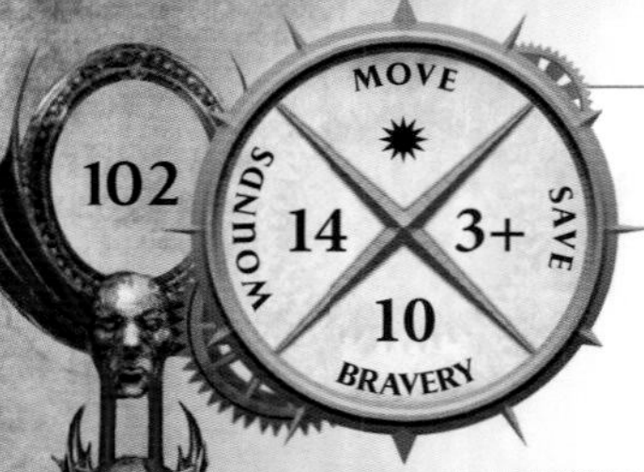

• WARSCROLL •

PRINCE VHORDRAI

From his macabre stronghold, the Crimson Keep, Prince Vhordrai leads his vampiric knights as they ride to war. Cursed for his past disloyalty, Vhordrai now serves as the Fist of Nagash, annihilating his master's enemies in displays of shocking violence.

MELEE WEAPONS	Range	Attacks	To Hit	To Wound	Rend	Damage
Bloodlance	2"	4	3+	3+	-2	2
Snapping Maw	3"	3	4+	3+	-2	D6
Sword-like Claws	2"	✸	4+	3+	-1	2

DAMAGE TABLE			
Wounds Suffered	Move	Breath of Shyish	Sword-like Claws
0-3	14"	D6	7
4-6	12"	D6	6
7-9	10"	3	5
10-12	8"	D3	4
13+	6"	1	3

DESCRIPTION

Prince Vhordrai is a named character that is a single model. He is armed with the Bloodlance.

If this model is included in a Soulblight Gravelords army with the **Kastelai Dynasty** lineage keyword, this model is treated as a general in addition to the model that is chosen to be the army general.

MOUNT: Prince Vhordrai's Zombie Dragon, Shordemaire, attacks with its Snapping Maw and Sword-like Claws.

FLY: Prince Vhordrai can fly.

ABILITIES

The Hunger: *Soulblight creatures crave the taste of blood and are empowered when they drink deep from the veins of defeated foes.*

At the end of the combat phase, if any enemy models were slain by wounds inflicted by this model's attacks in that phase, you can heal up to D3 wounds allocated to this model.

Chalice of Blood: *To sup from this ancient goblet will temporarily quench the bloody thirsts of its bearer.*

Once per battle, in your hero phase, you can heal up to D6 wounds allocated to this model.

Bloodlance Charge: *This ancient lance is even more deadly when wielded on the charge.*

Add 2 to the Damage characteristic of this model's Bloodlance and improve the Rend characteristic of that weapon by 1 if this model made a charge move in the same turn.

Breath of Shyish: *The undead drake Shordemaire can unleash a cloud of amethyst energies that see even the mightiest warriors drop dead in moments.*

In your shooting phase, you can pick 1 enemy unit within 9" of this model that is visible to it and roll a dice. On a 3+, that unit suffers a number of mortal wounds equal to the Breath of Shyish value shown on this model's damage table.

MAGIC

Prince Vhordrai is a **Wizard**. He can attempt to cast 1 spell in your hero phase and attempt to unbind 1 spell in the enemy hero phase. He knows the Arcane Bolt, Mystic Shield and Quickblood spells.

Quickblood: *Prince Vhordrai calls upon the power of the ancient curse running through his veins, lending strength and shocking speed to his strikes.*

Quickblood has a casting value of 7. If successfully cast, add 1 to hit and wound rolls for attacks made with melee weapons by the caster until your next hero phase.

COMMAND ABILITIES

Fist of Nagash: *Prince Vhordrai commands his servants to attack with unwavering focus, forbidding them to rest until all of Nagash's foes are destroyed*

You can use this command ability once per turn in your hero phase. If you do so, pick 1 other friendly **Soulblight Gravelords Hero** that is wholly within 12" of this model and within 3" of any enemy units. That **Hero** can fight.

KEYWORDS	DEATH, VAMPIRE, SOULBLIGHT GRAVELORDS, KASTELAI DYNASTY, ZOMBIE DRAGON, MONSTER, HERO, WIZARD, PRINCE VHORDRAI

• WARSCROLL •

PRINCE DUVALLE

Prince Duvalle claims descent from the von Carstein lineage, and few are foolish enough to gainsay him to his face. He is adept at conjuring magical glamours and illusions, rendering his prey disoriented and vulnerable before striking.

MELEE WEAPONS	Range	Attacks	To Hit	To Wound	Rend	Damage
Possessed Blade	1"	4	3+	3+	-1	2

DESCRIPTION

Prince Duvalle is a named character that is a single model. He is armed with a Possessed Blade.

ABILITIES

The Hunger: *Soulblight creatures crave the taste of blood and are empowered when they drink deep from the veins of defeated foes.*

At the end of the combat phase, if any enemy models were slain by wounds inflicted by this model's attacks in that phase, you can heal up to D3 wounds allocated to this model.

MAGIC

Prince Duvalle is a **WIZARD**. He can attempt to cast 1 spell in your hero phase and attempt to unbind 1 spell in the enemy hero phase. He knows the Arcane Bolt, Mystic Shield and Fiendish Lure spells.

Fiendish Lure: *Duvalle distorts the minds of his enemies with illusions of their fallen comrades, rendering them disoriented and vulnerable to the blades of the dead.*

Fiendish Lure has a casting value of 5. If successfully cast, pick 1 enemy unit within 6" of the caster that is visible to them. Add 1 to hit rolls for attacks that target that unit until your next hero phase.

KEYWORDS DEATH, VAMPIRE, SOULBLIGHT GRAVELORDS, HERO, WIZARD, PRINCE DUVALLE

• WARSCROLL •

THE CRIMSON COURT

Led by the charismatic Prince Duvalle, the Crimson Court are a clique of vampires obsessed with the hunt. Having slaked their thirsts the realms over, they now set their sights on the living mountain of Beastgrave and the warriors who battle within.

MELEE WEAPONS	Range	Attacks	To Hit	To Wound	Rend	Damage
Soulbound Mace	2"	2	3+	2+	-	D3
Paired Blades	1"	3	4+	3+	-1	1
Honed Bludgeon	1"	2	4+	3+	-	1

DESCRIPTION

The Crimson Court is a named unit that has 3 models. Gorath the Enforcer is armed with a Soulbound Mace; Vellas von Faine is armed with Paired Blades; and Ennias Curse-born is armed with a Honed Bludgeon.

GORATH THE ENFORCER: Add 2 to Gorath's Wounds characteristic.

ABILITIES

The Hunger: *Soulblight creatures crave the taste of blood and are empowered when they drink deep from the veins of defeated foes.*

At the end of the combat phase, if any enemy models were slain by wounds inflicted by this unit's attacks in that phase, you can heal up to D3 wounds allocated to this unit.

Vampiric Agility: *With quicksilver swiftness, these creatures can scale terrain in a matter of moments before pouncing upon their prey.*

When this unit makes a move, it can pass across terrain features in the same manner as a model that can fly.

KEYWORDS DEATH, VAMPIRE, SOULBLIGHT GRAVELORDS, THE CRIMSON COURT

• WARSCROLL •

LAUKA VAI

MOTHER OF NIGHTMARES

Lauka Vai is the queen of the Avengorii Dynasty. Within this monstrous vampire, an eternal battle rages, for though she desires to lead her kin against only the worthiest foes, her thirsts sometimes drive her to the most terrible slaughter.

MELEE WEAPONS	Range	Attacks	To Hit	To Wound	Rend	Damage
Askurga Rapier	1"	4	3+	3+	-1	2
Gore-drenched Talons	3"	3	4+	3+	-1	D6
Impaling Tail	1"	D6	4+	4+	-	1

DESCRIPTION

Lauka Vai is a named character that is a single model. She is armed with an Askurga Rapier, Gore-drenched Talons and Impaling Tail.

If this model is included in a Soulblight Gravelords army with the **AVENGORII DYNASTY** lineage keyword, this model is treated as a general in addition to the model that is chosen to be the army general.

FLY: Lauka Vai can fly.

ABILITIES

Champion of the Avengorii: *Lauka Vai's masterful martial prowess and monstrous beast-form render her an unholy terror upon the battlefield.*

After this model makes a charge move, you can pick 1 enemy unit within 1" of this model and roll a number of dice equal to the charge roll for that charge move. For each 5+, that enemy unit suffers 1 mortal wound.

Nightmare's Miasma: *The strange curse of the Vengorians sees shining blades and hallowed relics rust and soften in their presence.*

While an enemy unit is within 3" of any friendly models with this ability, worsen the Rend characteristic of that unit's melee weapons by 1 (to a minimum of '-').

Undeniable Impulse: *Lauka Vai fights a constant internal battle to control her bestial nature. It is not a battle she always wins.*

At the start of your hero phase, roll a dice for this model. If the roll is equal to or less than the number of the current battle round, until your next hero phase, this model can run and still charge later in the same turn. However, this model cannot use command abilities until your next hero phase.

The Hunger: *Soulblight creatures crave the taste of blood and are empowered when they drink deep from the veins of defeated foes.*

At the end of the combat phase, if any enemy models were slain by wounds inflicted by this model's attacks in that phase, you can heal up to D3 wounds allocated to this model.

MAGIC

Lauka Vai is a **WIZARD**. She can attempt to cast 1 spell in your hero phase and attempt to unbind 1 spell in the enemy hero phase. She knows the Arcane Bolt, Mystic Shield and Death's Downpour spells.

Death's Downpour: *Lauka draws upon the corrupt ending-magic running through her veins before lifting her blade skyward, summoning a deluge of slippery gore to wrong-foot her adversaries.*

Death's Downpour has a casting value of 8. If successfully cast, charge rolls made for enemy units within 12" of this model are halved until your next hero phase.

COMMAND ABILITIES

A Queen Amongst Monsters: *The Mother of Nightmares is followed by a menagerie of twisted vampires and monstrous undead beasts, all of whom seem empowered by her very presence.*

You can use this command ability once per turn in your hero phase. If you do so, pick 1 enemy unit on the battlefield. Until your next hero phase, add 1 to hit rolls for attacks made with melee weapons by friendly **SOULBLIGHT GRAVELORDS MONSTERS** that target that enemy unit.

KEYWORDS	DEATH, VAMPIRE, SOULBLIGHT GRAVELORDS, AVENGORII DYNASTY, MONSTER, HERO, WIZARD, LAUKA VAI

VENGORIAN LORD

Twisted by the power of unbound arcana, Vengorian Lords embody the nightmarish true nature of the Soulblight vampires. Unable to bear the sight of their own reflection, they wield magics of rust and clotting, revelling in their own self-loathing.

MELEE WEAPONS	Range	Attacks	To Hit	To Wound	Rend	Damage
Nightmare Sabre	1"	4	3+	3+	-1	2
Gore-drenched Talons	3"	3	4+	3+	-1	D6
Impaling Tail	1"	D6	4+	4+	-	1

DESCRIPTION

A Vengorian Lord is a single model armed with a Nightmare Sabre, Gore-drenched Talons and Impaling Tail.

FLY: This model can fly.

ABILITIES

Nightmare's Miasma: *The strange curse of the Vengorians sees shining blades and hallowed relics rust and soften in their presence.*

While an enemy unit is within 3" of any friendly models with this ability, worsen the Rend characteristic of that unit's melee weapons by 1 (to a minimum of '-').

Undeniable Impulse: *Many Vengorians struggle to hold onto their rationality, sometimes abandoning all pretence of command to indulge in wild, spiteful violence.*

At the start of your hero phase, roll a dice for this model. If the roll is equal to or less than the number of the current battle round, until your next hero phase, this model can run and still charge later in the same turn. However, this model cannot use command abilities until your next hero phase.

The Hunger: *Soulblight creatures crave the taste of blood and are empowered when they drink deep from the veins of defeated foes.*

At the end of the combat phase, if any enemy models were slain by wounds inflicted by this model's attacks in that phase, you can heal up to D3 wounds allocated to this model.

MAGIC

This model is a **WIZARD**. It can attempt to cast 1 spell in your hero phase and attempt to unbind 1 spell in the enemy hero phase. It knows the Arcane Bolt, Mystic Shield and Clotted Deluge spells.

Clotted Deluge: *The Vengorian summons a squall of foetid, clotted blood to splatter across a foe, focusing the attentions of nearby creatures of the night.*

Clotted Deluge has a casting value of 6. If successfully cast, pick 1 enemy unit within 12" of the caster that is visible to them. Add 1 to wound rolls for attacks made with melee weapons that target that unit until your next hero phase.

COMMAND ABILITIES

Festering Feast: *Vengorians bid their followers indulge in gory feasts even in the midst of battle. The more vile and unlovely the sight of the foe's blood, the more satisfying it is for these monsters.*

You can use this command ability at the end of the combat phase if any attacks made by a friendly **SOULBLIGHT GRAVELORDS** unit in that phase destroyed any enemy units. If you do so, you can heal up to D6 wounds allocated to that **SOULBLIGHT GRAVELORDS** unit. The same unit cannot benefit from this command ability more than once per phase.

KEYWORDS	DEATH, VAMPIRE, SOULBLIGHT GRAVELORDS, MONSTER, HERO, WIZARD, VENGORIAN LORD

• WARSCROLL •

BELLADAMMA VOLGA

FIRST OF THE VYRKOS

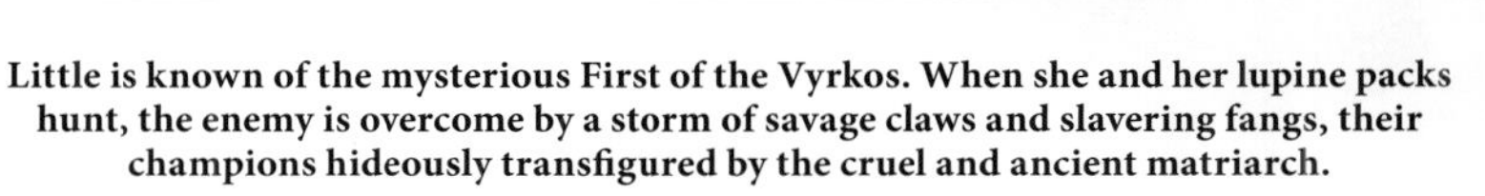

Little is known of the mysterious First of the Vyrkos. When she and her lupine packs hunt, the enemy is overcome by a storm of savage claws and slavering fangs, their champions hideously transfigured by the cruel and ancient matriarch.

MELEE WEAPONS	Range	Attacks	To Hit	To Wound	Rend	Damage
Timeworn Scimitar	1"	3	3+	3+	-1	D3
Lupine Fangs and Claws	1"	6	4+	4+	-	1

DESCRIPTION

Belladamma Volga is a named character that is a single model. She is armed with a Timeworn Scimitar.

If this model is included in a Soulblight Gravelords army with the **Vyrkos Dynasty** lineage keyword, this model is treated as a general in addition to the model that is chosen to be the army general.

MOUNT: Belladamma's wolves attack with their Lupine Fangs and Claws.

ABILITIES

The Hunger: *Soulblight creatures crave the taste of blood and are empowered when they drink deep from the veins of defeated foes.*

At the end of the combat phase, if any enemy models were slain by wounds inflicted by this model's attacks in that phase, you can heal up to D3 wounds allocated to this model.

First of the Vyrkos: *Belladamma wields all manner of strange and potent sorceries, many known only to the Elders of the Vyrkos. She uses these to bind packs of Dire Wolves to her service that will unthinkingly sacrifice themselves to protect their savage mistress.*

Add 1 to casting, dispelling and unbinding rolls for this model. In addition, roll a dice before you allocate a wound or mortal wound to this model if it is within 3" of any friendly **Dire Wolves** units. On a 3+, that wound or mortal wound is allocated to 1 of those units instead of this model.

MAGIC

Belladamma is a **Wizard**. She can attempt to cast 2 spells in your hero phase and attempt to unbind 2 spells in the enemy hero phase. She knows the Arcane Bolt, Mystic Shield, Lycancurse and Under a Killing Moon spells.

Lycancurse: *Singling out a choice foe, Belladamma's gnarled hand curls into a fist, lupine eyes watching as her victim's bones are crushed and warped into a form more pleasing to her.*

Lycancurse has a casting value of 7. If successfully cast, pick 1 enemy unit within 18" of the caster that is visible to them. That unit suffers D3 mortal wounds.

If any models in that unit were slain by this spell, before removing the last slain model, you can add 1 unit of **Dire Wolves** to your army. The number of models in the new unit must be equal to the number of models in the enemy unit that were slain by this spell. Set up the new unit within 3" of the slain model's unit, and then remove the slain model from play.

Under a Killing Moon: *The skies clear as a full and eerie moon rises to illuminate the battlefield. A synchronised howl echoes far and wide as the bestial warriors of the Vyrkos unleash their rage.*

Under a Killing Moon has a casting value of 6. If successfully cast, until your next hero phase, if the unmodified hit roll for an attack made with a melee weapon by a friendly **Soulblight Gravelords** unit wholly within 12" of the caster is 6, that attack inflicts 2 hits on the target instead of 1. Make a wound and save roll for each hit.

COMMAND ABILITIES

Pack Alpha: *The Dire Wolves of Belladamma's pack are amongst the most savage of their kind and will fall upon their foes with a slavering intensity.*

You can use this command ability at the start of your hero phase. If you do so, pick 1 friendly **Dire Wolves** unit wholly within 12" of this model. That unit is eligible to fight in the combat phase if it is within 6" of an enemy unit instead of 3", and it can move an extra 3" when it piles in.

KEYWORDS DEATH, VAMPIRE, SOULBLIGHT GRAVELORDS, VYRKOS DYNASTY, HERO, WIZARD, VAMPIRE LORD, BELLADAMMA VOLGA

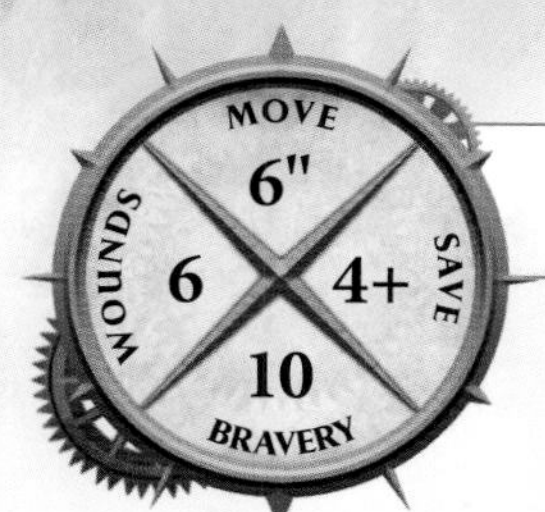

• WARSCROLL •

LADY ANNIKA

THE THIRSTING BLADE

Even amongst the Soulblight vampires, Lady Annika's thirst for blood is legendary. In battle, she attacks as a sanguine blur, her enchanted rapier reaping a red harvest as her foes fatally stumble and slip in the gore that inevitably pools about her feet.

MELEE WEAPONS	Range	Attacks	To Hit	To Wound	Rend	Damage
Blade Proboscian	1"	4	3+	3+	-1	D3

DESCRIPTION

Lady Annika is a named character that is a single model. She is armed with the Blade Proboscian.

If this model is included in a Soulblight Gravelords army with the **Vyrkos Dynasty** lineage keyword, this model is treated as a general in addition to the model that is chosen to be the army general.

ABILITIES

Supernatural Speed: *Many foes have mistaken Annika's slender form for an easy target, little appreciating the manic agility granted by her curse.*

Roll a dice each time you allocate a wound or mortal wound to this model. On a 4+, that wound or mortal wound is negated.

Kiss of the Blade Proboscian: *This pitted and corroded blade should not endure – and yet, it does. The same cannot be said for those even scratched by its mouldering point.*

At the end of a phase, if any enemy models were slain by wounds inflicted by this model's attacks in that phase, you can heal all wounds allocated to this model.

KEYWORDS DEATH, VAMPIRE, SOULBLIGHT GRAVELORDS, VYRKOS DYNASTY, HERO, VAMPIRE LORD, LADY ANNIKA

• WARSCROLL •

KRITZA

THE RAT PRINCE

Though Kritza professes nobility, in reality, his soul is as odious as the Ulfenkarni sewers that are his lair. Swathed in choking perfume, the Rat Prince is nevertheless a cunning adversary, returning after each apparent defeat to exact a cruel revenge.

MELEE WEAPONS	Range	Attacks	To Hit	To Wound	Rend	Damage
Gnawblade	1"	4	3+	3+	-1	D3

DESCRIPTION

Kritza is a named character that is a single model. He is armed with a Gnawblade.

If this model is included in a Soulblight Gravelords army with the **Vyrkos Dynasty** lineage keyword, this model is treated as a general in addition to the model that is chosen to be the army general.

ABILITIES

Scurrying Retreat: *Upon his apparent demise, Kritza will transfigure into a swarm of scurrying rats, only to rematerialise elsewhere and drive his blade into an unwary foe's back.*

If this model has been slain, at the end of your movement phase, roll a dice. On a 4+, a new model identical to the one that was slain is added to your army. Set up this model anywhere on the battlefield more than 9" from all enemy units.

Nauseating Aroma: *So thick are Kritza's perfumes, and so vile are they in nature, that even daemons have been known to be temporarily overwhelmed in his presence.*

Subtract 1 from hit rolls for attacks made with melee weapons that target this model.

KEYWORDS DEATH, VAMPIRE, SOULBLIGHT GRAVELORDS, VYRKOS DYNASTY, HERO, VAMPIRE LORD, KRITZA

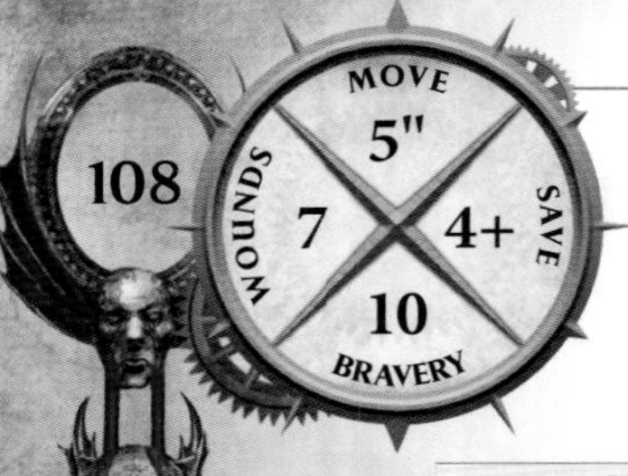

• WARSCROLL •

RADUKAR THE WOLF

Radukar is a cruel and savage vampire lord who rules over the city of Ulfenkarn. In battle, he wields the barrow-blade of a legendary vampire emperor, which, when combined with his bestial nature, makes Radukar a fearsome foe indeed.

MELEE WEAPONS	Range	Attacks	To Hit	To Wound	Rend	Damage
Vyrkos Barrow-blade	1"	4	3+	3+	-1	D3

DESCRIPTION

Radukar the Wolf is a named character that is a single model. He is armed with a Vyrkos Barrow-blade.

ABILITIES

The Hunger: *Soulblight creatures crave the taste of blood and are empowered when they drink deep from the veins of defeated foes.*

At the end of the combat phase, if any enemy models were slain by wounds inflicted by this model's attacks in that phase, you can heal up to D3 wounds allocated to this model.

Supernatural Strength: *When his bestial nature is let loose, Radukar can cleave foes in two with a strike of his mighty sword.*

If the unmodified wound roll for an attack made with a melee weapon by this model is 6, that attack inflicts 1 mortal wound on the target in addition to any normal damage.

Loyal to the Last: *To fight beside Radukar is an honour never taken lightly, and there are no guardians more selfless than the Kosargi Nightguard.*

Roll a dice before you allocate a wound or mortal wound to this model while it is within 3" of any friendly **KOSARGI NIGHTGUARD** units. On a 2+, that wound or mortal wound is allocated to 1 of those units instead of this model.

MAGIC

This model is a **WIZARD**. It can attempt to cast 1 spell in your hero phase and attempt to unbind 1 spell in the enemy hero phase. It knows the Arcane Bolt and Mystic Shield spells.

COMMAND ABILITIES

Call to the Hunt: *Radukar charges into the fray, calling upon all to cut down the foe before them.*

You can use this command ability at the start of the combat phase. If you do so, pick 1 friendly model with this command ability that made a charge move in that turn. Add 1 to the Attacks characteristic of melee weapons used by friendly **SOULBLIGHT GRAVELORDS** units wholly within 18" of that model until the end of that phase. The same unit cannot benefit from this command ability more than once per phase.

KEYWORDS	DEATH, VAMPIRE, SOULBLIGHT GRAVELORDS, VYRKOS DYNASTY, HERO, WIZARD, VAMPIRE LORD, RADUKAR THE WOLF

• WARSCROLL •

RADUKAR THE BEAST

Overwhelmed by his wrath, Radukar has undergone a terrifying transformation. The bestial monster within has come to consume the vampire almost entirely, and he now fights with a raw and brutal fury, his ferocious howls ringing through the night.

MELEE WEAPONS	Range	Attacks	To Hit	To Wound	Rend	Damage
Blood-slick Claws	2"	6	3+	3+	-1	2
Piercing Blade	1"	6	3+	3+	-1	D3

DESCRIPTION

Radukar the Beast is a named character that is a single model. He is armed with Blood-slick Claws.

If this model is included in a Soulblight Gravelords army with the **VYRKOS DYNASTY** lineage keyword, this model is treated as a general in addition to the model that is chosen to be the army general.

COMPANION: Radukar the Beast is accompanied by 2 Vyrkos Blood-born that attack with their Piercing Blades. For rules purposes, they are treated in the same manner as a mount.

ABILITIES

Bounding Charge: *Radukar's bestial form allows him to lope at shocking speed towards the enemy.*

This model can run and still charge later in the same turn.

The Hunger: *Soulblight creatures crave the taste of blood and are empowered when they drink deep from the veins of defeated foes.*

At the end of the combat phase, if any enemy models were slain by wounds inflicted by this model's attacks in that phase, you can heal up to D3 wounds allocated to this model.

Supernatural Reflexes: *In his more bestial state, Radukar's predatory instincts are honed to a razor's edge, rendering him almost impossible to strike.*

Subtract 1 from hit rolls for attacks that target this model.

Unleashed Ferocity: *The Beast's unnatural strength gives him terrifying power in melee combat.*

If the unmodified hit roll for an attack made with this model's Blood-slick Claws is 6, that attack inflicts 2 mortal wounds on the target and the attack sequence ends (do not make a wound or save roll).

COMMAND ABILITIES

Call to the Hunt: *Radukar charges into the fray, calling upon all to cut down the foe before them.*

You can use this command ability at the start of the combat phase. If you do so, pick 1 friendly model with this command ability that made a charge move in that turn. Add 1 to the Attacks characteristic of melee weapons used by friendly **SOULBLIGHT GRAVELORDS** units wholly within 18" of that model until the end of that phase. The same unit cannot benefit from this command ability more than once per phase.

Mustering Howl: *Radukar's howl is instantly recognisable. When released in the midst of battle, the resounding cry is met with an echoing chorus from his lupine kin.*

You can use this command ability once per battle at the end of your movement phase. If you do so, you can add 1 unit of 10 **DIRE WOLVES** to your army. The unit must be set up wholly within 12" of this model and more than 9" from all enemy units.

KEYWORDS	DEATH, VAMPIRE, SOULBLIGHT GRAVELORDS, VYRKOS DYNASTY, HERO, VAMPIRE LORD, RADUKAR THE BEAST

• WARSCROLL •

GORSLAV THE GRAVEKEEPER

The macabre creature known as Gorslav the Gravekeeper lords over the many cemeteries and mausoleums of Ulfenkarn. In battle, he leads hordes of shambling Deadwalkers that hurl themselves at the foe, infused with a rabid determination.

MELEE WEAPONS	Range	Attacks	To Hit	To Wound	Rend	Damage
Gravekeeper's Spade	2"	3	4+	3+	-1	D3

DESCRIPTION

Gorslav the Gravekeeper is a named character that is a single model. He is armed with a Gravekeeper's Spade.

ABILITIES

Keeper of the Corpse-gardens: *Those victims buried within the crypts and charnel pits of Ulfenkarn are bound to Gorslav through death magic. In battle, he can call upon his Deadwalker minions to throw themselves into enemy attacks and blunt their blades.*

Roll a dice before you allocate a wound or mortal wound to this model if it is within 3" of any friendly DEADWALKERS units. On a 4+, that wound or mortal wound is allocated to 1 of those units instead of this model.

COMMAND ABILITIES

Arise! Arise!: *With a rasping cry, the Gravekeeper beckons his freshly buried victims to arise once more in death and devour any living souls they find before them.*

You can use this command ability at the end of your movement phase. If you do so, pick 1 friendly SUMMONABLE DEADWALKERS unit that has been destroyed. A new replacement unit with half of the models from the unit that was destroyed (rounding up) is added to your army. Set up that unit wholly within 9" of a friendly model with this command ability and more than 9" from any enemy units. Each destroyed unit can only be replaced once – replacement units cannot themselves be replaced.

KEYWORDS	DEATH, SOULBLIGHT GRAVELORDS, VYRKOS DYNASTY, DEADWALKERS, HERO, GORSLAV THE GRAVEKEEPER

• WARSCROLL •

TORGILLIUS THE CHAMBERLAIN

This dark magician has earned himself a place in Radukar's court thanks to his mastery of grave-sand and its uses. When called into battle, Torgillius can unleash devastating sorcery that leaves any survivors drained of all strength.

MELEE WEAPONS	Range	Attacks	To Hit	To Wound	Rend	Damage
Claws and Fangs	1"	4	5+	4+	-	1

DESCRIPTION

Torgillius the Chamberlain is a named character that is a single model.

COMPANION: Torgillius the Chamberlain is accompanied by his vermin who attack with their Claws and Fangs. For rules purposes, they are treated in the same manner as a mount.

ABILITIES

Mastery of Grave-sand: *Torgillius can manipulate the energies of grave-sand to repel attackers.*

Roll a dice each time you allocate a wound or mortal wound to this unit. On a 4+, that wound or mortal wound is negated.

Trusted Lieutenant: *Radukar has granted Torgillius the resources with which to continue his research. In return, the Chamberlain provides his knowledge of necromancy and passes on the secrets gathered for him by his vermin spies.*

At the start of your hero phase, if this model is within 3" of a friendly RADUKAR THE WOLF, roll a dice. On a 4+, you receive 1 extra command point.

MAGIC

This model is a WIZARD. It can attempt to cast 1 spell in your hero phase and attempt to unbind 1 spell in the enemy hero phase. It knows the Arcane Bolt, Mystic Shield and Necrotising Bolt spells.

Necrotising Bolt: *Dark magic coalesces around Torgillius before being launched straight at the foe, sapping their strength and flaying soul from body.*

Necrotising Bolt has a casting value of 6. If successfully cast, pick 1 enemy unit within 18" of the caster that is visible to them. Subtract 1 from hit rolls for attacks made by that unit until your next hero phase.

KEYWORDS	DEATH, SOULBLIGHT GRAVELORDS, VYRKOS DYNASTY, DEATHMAGES, HERO, WIZARD, NECROMANCER, TORGILLIUS THE CHAMBERLAIN

WARSCROLL

VYRKOS BLOOD-BORN

In the gloom-shrouded streets of Ulfenkarn, the Vyrkos Blood-born are never far away, stalking the shadows in search of prey. Once these vampiric fiends catch the scent of blood, they attack with savage ferocity and lightning speed.

MELEE WEAPONS	Range	Attacks	To Hit	To Wound	Rend	Damage
Piercing Blade	1"	3	3+	3+	-1	D3

DESCRIPTION

A unit of Vyrkos Blood-born has any number of models, each armed with a Piercing Blade.

ABILITIES

Shadowfast: *Vyrkos Blood-born are able to dodge and deflect incoming blows with blurring speed.*

Roll a dice each time you allocate a wound or mortal wound to this unit. On a 5+, that wound or mortal wound is negated.

KEYWORDS DEATH, VAMPIRE, SOULBLIGHT GRAVELORDS, VYRKOS DYNASTY, VYRKOS BLOOD-BORN

WARSCROLL

WATCH CAPTAIN HALGRIM

During the purge of the city, the traitorous Watch Captain Oleksandr Halgrim was swift to swear himself and his warriors to the Wolf's cause. Now in death, he commands the vast legions of skeleton warriors known as the Ulfenwatch.

MELEE WEAPONS	Range	Attacks	To Hit	To Wound	Rend	Damage
Cursed Halberd	2"	3	4+	3+	-1	D3

DESCRIPTION

Watch Captain Halgrim is a named character that is a single model. He is armed with a Cursed Halberd.

ABILITIES

Cursed Halberd: *Foul necrotic sorcery clings to this ancient weapon.*

If the unmodified hit roll for an attack made with a Cursed Halberd is 6, that attack inflicts 1 mortal wound on the target in addition to any normal damage.

COMMAND ABILITIES

Disciplined Advance: *Under Halgrim's command, his warriors advance ceaselessly in regimented lockstep to crush the foes of Ulfenkarn.*

You can use this command ability at the start of your movement phase. If you do so, pick up to 3 friendly **DEATHRATTLE** units wholly within 18" of this model. Until the end of that phase, if you declare that any of those units will run, do not make a run roll for them. Instead, add 4" to the Move characteristic of those units until the end of that phase.

KEYWORDS DEATH, SOULBLIGHT GRAVELORDS, VYRKOS DYNASTY, DEATHRATTLE, HERO, WATCH CAPTAIN HALGRIM

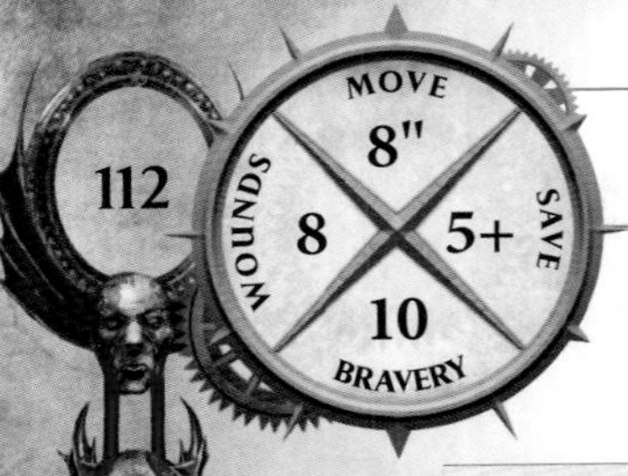

• WARSCROLL •

VARGSKYR

Unable to control the feral aspect of the curse that surges through their blood, Vargskyr are towering, distended creatures. On the hunt, they stalk their prey before descending upon them in a frenzy of slashing claws and razor-sharp fangs.

MELEE WEAPONS	Range	Attacks	To Hit	To Wound	Rend	Damage
Talons	2"	4	3+	3+	-1	2
Gaping Maw	1"	1	3+	2+	-2	D3

DESCRIPTION

A Vargskyr is a single model armed with Talons and a Gaping Maw.

ABILITIES

Bounding Leaps: *Three times the height of a man and with supernatural strength and reflexes, a Vargskyr covers ground with terrifying speed.*

You can attempt to charge with this model if it is within 18" of the enemy instead of 12". Roll 3D6 instead of 2D6 when making a charge roll for this model.

Gnarled Hide: *These savage beasts are covered in thick wiry fur and jutting bones that act as natural armour.*

Roll a dice each time you allocate a wound or mortal wound to this model. On a 5+, that wound or mortal wound is negated.

KEYWORDS DEATH, VAMPIRE, SOULBLIGHT GRAVELORDS, VYRKOS DYNASTY, VARGSKYR

• WARSCROLL •

KOSARGI NIGHTGUARD

The Kosargi ogors have served Radukar for centuries, first in life and now in death, raised from the grave with foul necrotic sorcery. In battle, they scatter all foes before them, carving great bloody swathes into the enemy with each swing of their bardiches.

MELEE WEAPONS	Range	Attacks	To Hit	To Wound	Rend	Damage
Bardiche	2"	2	3+	3+	-1	2

DESCRIPTION

A unit of Kosargi Nightguard has any number of models, each armed with a Bardiche.

ABILITIES

Deathly Vigour: *The rotting flesh of these lumbering brutes can absorb even the most grievous of wounds dealt to them.*

Roll a dice each time you allocate a wound or mortal wound to this unit. On a 5+, that wound or mortal wound is negated.

Servants Even in Death: *These formidable undead ogors are as utterly loyal to Radukar as they were in life.*

Add 1 to the Attacks characteristic of this unit's Bardiches while it is wholly within 12" of a friendly **RADUKAR THE WOLF**.

KEYWORDS DEATH, OGOR, SOULBLIGHT GRAVELORDS, VYRKOS DYNASTY, DEADWALKERS, KOSARGI NIGHTGUARD

• WARSCROLL •

VAMPIRE LORD

ON ZOMBIE DRAGON

The proudest and most martial of vampires take to battle astride terrifying undead drakes. Armed with such a potent mount, they are capable of turning the tide of battle alone, striking down their rivals and supping their blood from enchanted goblets.

MISSILE WEAPONS	Range	Attacks	To Hit	To Wound	Rend	Damage
Pestilential Breath	9"	1	3+	✹	-3	D6
MELEE WEAPONS	**Range**	**Attacks**	**To Hit**	**To Wound**	**Rend**	**Damage**
Deathlance	1"	3	3+	3+	-1	2
Vampiric Sword	1"	4	3+	3+	-1	D3
Snapping Maw	3"	3	4+	3+	-2	D6
Sword-like Claws	2"	✹	4+	3+	-1	2

DAMAGE TABLE			
Wounds Suffered	**Move**	**Pestilential Breath**	**Sword-like Claws**
0-3	14"	2+	7
4-6	12"	3+	6
7-9	10"	4+	5
10-12	8"	5+	4
13+	6"	6+	3

DESCRIPTION

A Vampire Lord on Zombie Dragon is a single model armed with 1 of the following weapon options: Deathlance; or Vampiric Sword.

MOUNT: This model's Zombie Dragon attacks with its Pestilential Breath, Snapping Maw and Sword-like Claws.

FLY: This model can fly.

ABILITIES

Pestilential Breath: *When a Zombie Dragon looses its breath, the killing miasma withers flesh and saps life from the living.*

When you attack with this model's Pestilential Breath, roll a dice before making the hit roll for the attack. If the roll is less than or equal to the number of models in the target unit, the attack scores a hit without needing to make a hit roll.

The Hunger: *Soulblight creatures crave the taste of blood and are empowered when they drink deep from the veins of defeated foes.*

At the end of the combat phase, if any enemy models were slain by wounds inflicted by this model's attacks in that phase, you can heal up to D3 wounds allocated to this model.

Deathlance Charge: *A Deathlance can inflict hideous wounds when wielded with sufficient momentum.*

Add 2 to the Damage characteristic of this model's Deathlance and improve the Rend characteristic of that weapon by 1 if this model made a charge move in the same turn.

MAGIC

This model is a **WIZARD**. It can attempt to cast 1 spell in your hero phase and attempt to unbind 1 spell in the enemy hero phase. It knows the Arcane Bolt, Mystic Shield and Curse of Exsanguination spells.

Curse of Exsanguination: *Speaking an incantation from the Sixth Book of Nagash, the vampire commands an enemy's blood to violently burst from their body.*

Curse of Exsanguination has a casting value of 6. If successfully cast, pick 1 enemy unit within 18" of the caster that is visible to them. That unit suffers 1 mortal wound. If that mortal wound is allocated to a model in that unit and not negated and that model is not slain by that mortal wound, you can roll a dice. On a 4+, that model suffers 1 mortal wound, and you can roll another dice if that mortal wound is allocated and not negated and the model is not slain. Keep rolling dice in this way until either no mortal wounds are inflicted, the mortal wound is negated or the model is slain.

KEYWORDS	DEATH, VAMPIRE, SOULBLIGHT GRAVELORDS, ZOMBIE DRAGON, MONSTER, HERO, WIZARD, VAMPIRE LORD

• WARSCROLL •

BLOOD KNIGHTS

Blood Knights are vampires obsessed with battle, and their codes of chivalric honour are warped indeed. Mounted atop hulking Nightmares, they seek out war wherever it can be found, trampling straight over lesser foes to reach the worthiest challenges.

MELEE WEAPONS	Range	Attacks	To Hit	To Wound	Rend	Damage
Templar Lance or Blade	1"	3	3+	3+	-1	1
Hooves and Teeth	1"	3	4+	4+	-	1

DESCRIPTION

A unit of Blood Knights has any number of models, each armed with a Templar Lance or Blade.

MOUNT: This unit's Nightmares attack with their Hooves and Teeth.

CHAMPION: 1 model in this unit can be a Kastellan. Add 1 to the Attacks characteristic of a Kastellan's Templar Lance or Blade.

STANDARD BEARER: 1 in every 5 models in this unit can be a Standard Bearer. You can re-roll rolls of 1 for the Deathless Minions battle trait for this unit while it has any Standard Bearers.

ABILITIES

Riders of Ruin: *Blood Knights trample clean over lesser foes to strike at more worthy challengers.*

In your movement phase, if this unit is within 3" of an enemy unit, it can make a normal move. If it does so, it can pass across other models with a Wounds characteristic of 3 or less (that do not have a mount) in the same manner as a model that can fly. After this unit has made a normal move, roll a dice for each enemy unit that has any models passed across by any models in this unit. On a 2+, that enemy unit suffers D3 mortal wounds.

Martial Fury: *Woe betide any who dare stand before a Blood Knight's charge.*

Add 1 to the Damage characteristic of this unit's Templar Lances or Blades if this unit made a charge move in the same turn.

The Hunger: *Soulblight creatures crave the taste of blood and are empowered when they drink deep from the veins of defeated foes.*

At the end of the combat phase, if any enemy models were slain by wounds inflicted by this unit's attacks in that phase, you can heal up to D3 wounds allocated to this unit.

KEYWORDS	DEATH, VAMPIRE, SOULBLIGHT GRAVELORDS, BLOOD KNIGHTS

• WARSCROLL •

VARGHEISTS

The leather-winged horrors known as Vargheists are vampires who were overwhelmed by their bloody thirsts. Now reduced to savage and near-uncontrollable beasts, they viciously attack any prey in sight in a flurry of tearing claws and sharp fangs.

MELEE WEAPONS	Range	Attacks	To Hit	To Wound	Rend	Damage
Murderous Fangs and Talons	1"	3	3+	3+	-1	2

DESCRIPTION

A unit of Vargheists has any number of models, each armed with Murderous Fangs and Talons.

FLY: This unit can fly.

CHAMPION: 1 model in this unit can be a Vargoyle. Add 1 to the Attacks characteristic of a Vargoyle's Murderous Fangs and Talons.

ABILITIES

Blood-maddened Feeding Frenzy: *The taste of blood sends these murderous horrors into a savage killing frenzy.*

If the unmodified hit roll for an attack made by this unit is 6, that attack scores 2 hits on the target instead of 1. Make a wound and save roll for each hit.

Death's Descent: *Vargheists favour swooping down at their victims from on high, suddenly overwhelming them in a flurry of claws and fangs.*

Instead of setting up this unit on the battlefield, you can place it to one side and say that it is circling high above as a reserve unit. If you do so, at the end of your movement phase, you can set up this unit on the battlefield more than 9" from any enemy units. At the start of the fourth battle round, any models that are still in reserve are slain.

KEYWORDS	DEATH, VAMPIRE, SOULBLIGHT GRAVELORDS, VARGHEISTS

• WARSCROLL •

VAMPIRE LORD

MOVE	WOUNDS	SAVE	BRAVERY
6"	5	3+	10

116

Vampire Lords are elder undead whose dark powers have only deepened over the long centuries. Each is a warrior to be feared, while their command of necromancy sees them raise up fresh reanimated warriors with but a pulse of will.

MELEE WEAPONS	Range	Attacks	To Hit	To Wound	Rend	Damage
Soulbound Blades	1"	4	3+	3+	-1	D3

DESCRIPTION

A Vampire Lord is a single model armed with Soulbound Blades.

FLY: This model can fly.

ABILITIES

The Hunger: *Soulblight creatures crave the taste of blood and are empowered when they drink deep from the veins of defeated foes.*

At the end of the combat phase, if any enemy models were slain by wounds inflicted by this model's attacks in that phase, you can heal up to D3 wounds allocated to this model.

MAGIC

This model is a **WIZARD**. It can attempt to cast 1 spell in your hero phase and attempt to unbind 1 spell in the enemy hero phase. It knows the Arcane Bolt and Mystic Shield spells.

COMMAND ABILITIES

Crimson Feast: *The Vampire Lord unshackles the monstrous bloodlust that lurks within their soul, their bestial appetites soon spreading to the undead bound to their will.*

You can use this command ability in the combat phase. If you do so, pick 1 friendly **SOULBLIGHT GRAVELORDS SUMMONABLE** unit wholly within 12" of this model. Add 1 to the Attacks characteristic of that unit's melee weapons until your next hero phase. The same unit cannot benefit from this command ability more than once per phase.

KEYWORDS	DEATH, VAMPIRE, SOULBLIGHT GRAVELORDS, HERO, WIZARD, VAMPIRE LORD

BLOODSEEKER PALANQUIN

From atop macabre conveyances known as Bloodseeker Palanquins, the Sanguinarchs refine the art of blood-blending. In battle, they violently exsanguinate worthy champions, using their ichor in crimson concoctions to invigorate their vampiric kin.

MISSILE WEAPONS	Range	Attacks	To Hit	To Wound	Rend	Damage
Wail of the Damned	✹			See below		
MELEE WEAPONS	**Range**	**Attacks**	**To Hit**	**To Wound**	**Rend**	**Damage**
Bloodletting Blade	1"	4	3+	3+	-1	D3
Spectral Claws and Blades	1"	✹	5+	4+	-	1

DAMAGE TABLE			
Wounds Suffered	**Move**	**Wail of the Damned**	**Spectral Claws and Blades**
0-2	14"	12"	12
3-4	12"	10"	10
5-7	10"	8"	8
8-9	8"	6"	6
10+	6"	4"	4

DESCRIPTION

A Bloodseeker Palanquin is a single model ridden by a Sanguinarch armed with a Bloodletting Blade.

MOUNT: This model's Spectral Host attacks with their Wail of the Damned and Spectral Claws and Blades.

FLY: This model can fly.

ABILITIES

A Fine Vintage: *Sanguinarchs are obsessed with sampling the finest blood vintages and can further refine and blend such rich pickings to augment their followers.*

If an enemy HERO is slain within 9" of this model, add 1 to the Attacks characteristic of melee weapons used by friendly VAMPIRE units wholly within 12" of this model until your next hero phase.

Frightful Touch: *The malign spirits that surround the Bloodseeker Palanquin can freeze an opponent's blood with a single touch.*

If the unmodified hit roll for an attack made with this model's Spectral Claws and Blades is 6, that attack inflicts 1 mortal wound on the target and the attack sequence ends (do not make a wound or save roll).

Wail of the Damned: *Unnerving howls follow this carriage wherever it roams. Should an enemy get close enough, the spectral host unleashes a deafening wail that tears the soul apart.*

Do not use the attack sequence for an attack made with a Wail of the Damned. Instead, roll a dice for each enemy unit within range of this model's Wail of the Damned. On a 4+, that unit suffers D3 mortal wounds.

MAGIC

This model is a WIZARD. It can attempt to cast 1 spell in your hero phase and attempt to unbind 1 spell in the enemy hero phase. It knows the Arcane Bolt, Mystic Shield and Blood Siphon spells.

Blood Siphon: *With a contemptuous gesture, the Sanguinarch calls forth a torrent of blood from their victim's eyes, nose and mouth.*

Blood Siphon has a casting value of 6. If successfully cast, pick 1 enemy HERO within 12" of the caster that is visible to them and roll a dice. On a 1-2, the target suffers 1 mortal wound. On a 3-4, the target suffers D3 mortal wounds. On a 5-6, the target suffers D6 mortal wounds.

KEYWORDS	DEATH, VAMPIRE, MALIGNANT, SOULBLIGHT GRAVELORDS, HERO, WIZARD, BLOODSEEKER PALANQUIN

MORTIS ENGINE

Within each Mortis Engine is bound the remains of a powerful liche-lord. Death magic is drawn to these constructs, a reservoir of power that can be tapped into by fellow practitioners or else unleashed in a burst of lethal energy.

MISSILE WEAPONS	Range	Attacks	To Hit	To Wound	Rend	Damage
Wail of the Damned	✷			See below		
MELEE WEAPONS	**Range**	**Attacks**	**To Hit**	**To Wound**	**Rend**	**Damage**
Mortis Staff	1"	2	4+	3+	-1	D3
Spectral Claws and Blades	1"	✷	5+	4+	-	1

DAMAGE TABLE			
Wounds Suffered	**Move**	**Wail of the Damned**	**Spectral Claws and Blades**
0-2	14"	12"	12
3-4	12"	10"	10
5-7	10"	8"	8
8-9	8"	6"	6
10+	6"	4"	4

DESCRIPTION

A Mortis Engine is a single model driven by a Corpsemaster armed with a Mortis Staff.

MOUNT: This model's Spectral Host attacks with their Wail of the Damned and Spectral Claws and Blades.

FLY: This model can fly.

ABILITIES

Frightful Touch: *The malign spirits that surround the Mortis Engine can freeze an opponent's blood with a single touch.*

If the unmodified hit roll for an attack made with this model's Spectral Claws and Blades is 6, that attack inflicts 1 mortal wound on the target and the attack sequence ends (do not make a wound or save roll).

Wail of the Damned: *Unnerving howls follow this carriage wherever it roams. Should an enemy get close enough, the spectral host unleashes a deafening wail that tears the soul apart.*

Do not use the attack sequence for an attack made with a Wail of the Damned. Instead, roll a dice for each enemy unit within range of this model's Wail of the Damned. On a 4+, that unit suffers D3 mortal wounds.

The Reliquary: *The Corpsemaster custodian of a Mortis Engine can unleash the thrumming amethyst magics that surge through it in a lethal shockwave.*

Once per battle, in your hero phase, you can say that this model will unleash the energies of its reliquary. If you do so, roll a dice for each unit within 12" of this model. On a 2+, that unit suffers D3 mortal wounds. **DEATH** units are not affected by this ability.

Bound Necromancer: *Mortis Engines are constructed around the remains of a slain master Necromancer, who acts as a locus of forbidden power for other undead to draw upon.*

Add 1 to casting rolls for friendly **SOULBLIGHT GRAVELORDS WIZARDS** wholly within 12" of any friendly models with this ability.

KEYWORDS	DEATH, MALIGNANT, SOULBLIGHT GRAVELORDS, DEATHMAGES, MORTIS ENGINE

• WARSCROLL •

COVEN THRONE

From atop the morbid Coven Thrones, a Vampire Lady and her acolytes mark the most intriguing foes. Those chosen are beguiled even as they are torn asunder, their blood drained into a mystical font and used to scry the tangled paths to victory.

MELEE WEAPONS	Range	Attacks	To Hit	To Wound	Rend	Damage
Predatory Bite	1"	1	3+	3+	-	D3
Stiletto	1"	4	3+	3+	-1	1
Needle-sharp Poniards	1"	✹	3+	3+	-	1
Spectral Claws and Blades	1"	✹	5+	4+	-	1

DAMAGE TABLE			
Wounds Suffered	Move	Needle-sharp Poniards	Spectral Claws and Blades
0-2	14"	8	12
3-4	12"	7	10
5-7	10"	6	8
8-9	8"	5	6
10+	6"	4	4

DESCRIPTION

A Coven Throne is a single model ridden by a Vampire Lady armed with a Predatory Bite and Stiletto.

MOUNT: This model's Spectral Host attacks with their Spectral Claws and Blades.

COMPANION: This model is accompanied by Handmaidens who attack with their Needle-sharp Poniards. For rules purposes, they are treated in the same manner as a mount.

FLY: This model can fly.

ABILITIES

The Hunger: *Soulblight creatures crave the taste of blood and are empowered when they drink deep from the veins of defeated foes.*

At the end of the combat phase, if any enemy models were slain by wounds inflicted by this model's attacks in that phase, you can heal up to D3 wounds allocated to this model.

Frightful Touch: *The malign spirits that surround the Coven Throne can freeze an opponent's blood with a single touch.*

If the unmodified hit roll for an attack made with this model's Spectral Claws and Blades is 6, that attack inflicts 1 mortal wound on the target and the attack sequence ends (do not make a wound or save roll).

Scrying Pool: *Within this pool of shimmering, enchanted gore, the Vampire Lady foresees the shape of the battle to come.*

Once per turn, you can re-roll 1 hit roll or 1 wound roll for an attack made by this model or 1 save roll for an attack that targets this model.

MAGIC

This model is a **WIZARD**. It can attempt to cast 1 spell in your hero phase and attempt to unbind 1 spell in the enemy hero phase. It knows the Arcane Bolt, Mystic Shield and Shudder spells.

Shudder: *Staring into their eyes, the caster clouds her prey's mind and instils fear into their heart.*

Shudder has a casting value of 6. If successfully cast, pick 1 enemy unit within 12" of the caster that is visible to them and roll 3D6. If the roll is greater than that unit's Bravery characteristic, this model cannot be picked to be the target of any attacks made, spells cast or abilities used by that unit until your next hero phase.

COMMAND ABILITIES

Tactical Insight: *The Vampire Lady and her Handmaidens employ their divinatory abilities to manipulate and aid their undying servants.*

You can use this command ability at the start of your hero phase. If you do so, pick 1 friendly **SOULBLIGHT GRAVELORDS** unit wholly within 12" of this model. Until your next hero phase, add 1 to hit rolls and wound rolls for attacks made by that unit and add 1 to save rolls for attacks that target that unit. The same unit cannot benefit from this command ability more than once per phase.

KEYWORDS | DEATH, VAMPIRE, MALIGNANT, SOULBLIGHT GRAVELORDS, HERO, WIZARD, COVEN THRONE

• WARSCROLL •

NECROMANCER

Necromancers are those mortals who, in their quest to attain mastery over death, wield the foulest Shyishan magics. At their command, the undead rise from their graves, granted an unholy impetus by their masters even as they shield them from harm.

MELEE WEAPONS	Range	Attacks	To Hit	To Wound	Rend	Damage
Mortis Staff	1"	2	3+	3+	-1	D3

DESCRIPTION

A Necromancer is a single model armed with a Mortis Staff.

ABILITIES

Undead Minions: *The Necromancer pulls servants of death into harm's way to protect the flow of their reanimating magic*

Roll a dice before you allocate a wound or mortal wound to this model if it is within 3" of any friendly **Soulblight Gravelords Summonable** units. On a 3+, that wound or mortal wound is allocated to 1 of those units instead of this model.

MAGIC

This model is a **Wizard**. It can attempt to cast 1 spell in your hero phase and attempt to unbind 1 spell in the enemy hero phase. It knows the Arcane Bolt, Mystic Shield and Vanhel's Danse Macabre spells.

Vanhel's Danse Macabre: *The undead are filled with magical energy that causes them to jerk forwards and attack with tireless, unnatural speed.*

Vanhel's Danse Macabre has a casting value of 6. If successfully cast, pick 1 friendly **Soulblight Gravelords Summonable** unit wholly within 18" of the caster. Until your next hero phase, if that unit has fought only once in the combat phase, when it is your turn to pick a unit to fight, that unit can be picked to fight for a second time if it is within 3" of any enemy units.

KEYWORDS DEATH, SOULBLIGHT GRAVELORDS, DEATHMAGES, HERO, WIZARD, NECROMANCER

• WARSCROLL •

DEADWALKER ZOMBIES

Deadwalker Zombies are the resurrected corpses of the recently slain. Though individually weak, in great numbers, they can overwhelm even the mightiest warriors – and those whom they slay are liable to rise as Deadwalkers themselves.

MELEE WEAPONS	Range	Attacks	To Hit	To Wound	Rend	Damage
Crude Weapons and Infectious Bites	1"	1	5+	5+	-	1

DESCRIPTION

A unit of Deadwalker Zombies has any number of models, each armed with Crude Weapons and Infectious Bites.

ABILITIES

Dragged Down and Torn Apart: *Though Deadwalker Zombies are clumsy and slow, they should never be underestimated, for when the foe is near, they can move with an ungainly but disturbingly determined gait.*

This unit is eligible to fight in the combat phase if it is within 6" of an enemy unit instead of 3", and it can move an extra 3" when it piles in.

The Newly Dead: *Those who fall to a zombie's bite soon rise to join the unliving horde.*

If the unmodified hit roll for an attack made by this unit is 6, that attack inflicts 1 mortal wound on the target and the attack sequence ends. In addition, at the end of the combat phase, you can roll a dice for each enemy model that was slain by wounds inflicted by this unit's attacks in that phase. For each 2+, you can add 1 **Deadwalker Zombie** model to this unit.

KEYWORDS DEATH, SOULBLIGHT GRAVELORDS, DEADWALKERS, SUMMONABLE, DEADWALKER ZOMBIES

• WARSCROLL •

CORPSE CART

WITH UNHOLY LODESTONE

Corpse Carts are rattling, mobile altars of undeath pulled by moaning Deadwalkers. The cackling of the Corpsemaster echoes over the tolling of black-iron bells, while the necrotic aura surrounding them sees the dead rise to their feet once more.

MELEE WEAPONS	Range	Attacks	To Hit	To Wound	Rend	Damage
Corpse Goad	2"	2	4+	4+	-	1
Corpse Lash	1"	3	4+	4+	-	1
Rusty Blades	1"	2D6	5+	5+	-	1

DESCRIPTION

A Corpse Cart with Unholy Lodestone is a single model driven by a Corpsemaster armed with 1 of the following weapon options: Corpse Goad; or Corpse Lash.

MOUNT: This model's Zombies attack with their Rusty Blades.

ABILITIES

Unholy Lodestone: *These sinister relics serve to attract and empower the sinister magical energies wielded by the Soulblight Gravelords.*

Add 1 to casting rolls for friendly **Soulblight Gravelords Wizards** wholly within 12" of any friendly models with this ability.

Locus of Undeath: *Many Corpse Carts are veritable wellsprings of necromantic power that can be drawn upon to replenish the ranks of the living dead.*

Add 1 to save rolls for attacks that target friendly **Deadwalker Zombies** units wholly within 12" of any friendly models with this ability.

KEYWORDS DEATH, SOULBLIGHT GRAVELORDS, DEADWALKERS, CORPSE CART, CORPSE CART WITH UNHOLY LODESTONE

• WARSCROLL •

CORPSE CART

WITH BALEFIRE BRAZIER

Some Corpse Carts are crowned with rusted braziers in which realmstone is burnt upon unhallowed flames. The choking clouds that emerge from these constructs snuff out the power of the aether and can drive mages mad with but a single inhalation.

MELEE WEAPONS	Range	Attacks	To Hit	To Wound	Rend	Damage
Corpse Goad	2"	2	4+	4+	-	1
Corpse Lash	1"	3	4+	4+	-	1
Rusty Blades	1"	2D6	5+	5+	-	1

DESCRIPTION

A Corpse Cart with Balefire Brazier is a single model driven by a Corpsemaster armed with 1 of the following weapon options: Corpse Goad; or Corpse Lash.

MOUNT: This model's Zombies attack with their Rusty Blades.

ABILITIES

Balefire Brazier: *The corrupt realmstone burnt upon these rusted braziers release gouts of ominous mist that, when breathed in, can drive enemy sorcerers to madness.*

Subtract 1 from casting rolls for enemy **Wizards** within 18" of any friendly models with this ability.

Malefic Fumes: *An unholy stench surrounds these creaking wagons, choking and disorienting nearby foes.*

Subtract 1 from wound rolls for attacks made with melee weapons by enemy units while they are within 9" of any friendly models with this ability.

KEYWORDS DEATH, SOULBLIGHT GRAVELORDS, DEADWALKERS, CORPSE CART, CORPSE CART WITH BALEFIRE BRAZIER

• WARSCROLL •

ZOMBIE DRAGON

With a deafening roar, the Zombie Dragon dives into battle, eye sockets aglow with necromantic energy. The beast shreds flesh, bone and steel with equal ease, its talons and maw matched in their lethality only by its billowing pestilential breath.

MISSILE WEAPONS	Range	Attacks	To Hit	To Wound	Rend	Damage
Pestilential Breath	9"	1	3+	✹	-3	D6
MELEE WEAPONS	**Range**	**Attacks**	**To Hit**	**To Wound**	**Rend**	**Damage**
Snapping Maw	3"	3	4+	3+	-2	D6
Sword-like Claws	2"	✹	4+	3+	-1	2

DAMAGE TABLE			
Wounds Suffered	**Move**	**Pestilential Breath**	**Sword-like Claws**
0-3	14"	2+	7
4-6	12"	3+	6
7-9	10"	4+	5
10-12	8"	5+	4
13+	6"	6+	3

DESCRIPTION

A Zombie Dragon is a single model armed with Pestilential Breath, a Snapping Maw and Sword-like Claws.

FLY: This model can fly.

ABILITIES

Pestilential Breath: *When a Zombie Dragon looses its breath, the killing miasma withers flesh and saps life from the living.*

When you attack with this model's Pestilential Breath, roll a dice before making the hit roll for the attack. If the roll is less than or equal to the number of models in the target unit, the attack scores a hit without needing to make a hit roll.

KEYWORDS	DEATH, SOULBLIGHT GRAVELORDS, MONSTER, ZOMBIE DRAGON

• WARSCROLL •

TERRORGHEIST

The Terrorgheist is a bloodthirsty undead beast whose piercing cry scythes through the enemy as it plunges into the fray. Should the creature be slain, another horror awaits its foes, as hundreds of shrieking bats burst from its remains to ravage those nearby.

MISSILE WEAPONS	Range	Attacks	To Hit	To Wound	Rend	Damage
Death Shriek	10"	1	See below			
MELEE WEAPONS	**Range**	**Attacks**	**To Hit**	**To Wound**	**Rend**	**Damage**
Fanged Maw	3"	3	4+	3+	-2	D6
Skeletal Claws	2"	✹	4+	3+	-1	D3

DAMAGE TABLE			
Wounds Suffered	**Move**	**Death Shriek**	**Skeletal Claws**
0-3	14"	6	4
4-6	12"	5	4
7-9	10"	4	3
10-12	8"	3	3
13+	6"	2	2

DESCRIPTION

A Terrorgheist is a single model armed with a Death Shriek, Fanged Maw and Skeletal Claws.

FLY: This model can fly.

ABILITIES

Death Shriek: *The terrifying shriek of a Terrorgheist is enough to stop a warrior's heart.*

Do not use the attack sequence for an attack made with this model's Death Shriek. Instead, roll a dice and add the Death Shriek value shown on this model's damage table. If the total is higher than the target unit's Bravery characteristic, the target unit suffers a number of mortal wounds equal to the difference between its Bravery characteristic and the total.

Gaping Maw: *This horrific creature bites a great chunk out of its prey – or even swallows it whole.*

If the unmodified hit roll for an attack made with this model's Fanged Maw is 6, that attack inflicts 6 mortal wounds on the target and the attack sequence ends (do not make a wound or save roll).

Infested: *When a Terrorgheist is finally destroyed, it explodes into a swarm of bats that feast on those nearby.*

If this model is slain, before this model is removed from play, each unit within 3" of this model suffers D3 mortal wounds.

KEYWORDS	DEATH, SOULBLIGHT GRAVELORDS, MONSTER, TERRORGHEIST

• WARSCROLL •

WIGHT KING

Wight Kings are the rulers of the Deathrattle nations, warrior-lords whose souls still lust for conquest. Though their flesh has rotted away, their tactical acumen endures, and at their command, regiments of skeletal soldiery attack with redoubled fervour.

MELEE WEAPONS	Range	Attacks	To Hit	To Wound	Rend	Damage
Baleful Tomb Blade	1"	4	3+	3+	-1	D3

DESCRIPTION

A Wight King is a single model armed with a Baleful Tomb Blade.

ABILITIES

Beheading Strike: *The cursed blades wielded by the most lordly Wights can kill with a single cut.*

If the unmodified hit roll for an attack made with this model's Baleful Tomb Blade is 6, the target suffers 1 mortal wound in addition to any normal damage.

COMMAND ABILITIES

Lord of Bones: *At the rasped command of their king, the Deathrattle hordes lay about the enemy with a tireless focus.*

You can use this command ability in your hero phase. If you do so, pick 1 friendly DEATHRATTLE unit wholly within 12" of this model. Until the end of that phase, you can re-roll hit rolls of 1 for attacks made with melee weapons by that unit.

KEYWORDS DEATH, SOULBLIGHT GRAVELORDS, DEATHRATTLE, HERO, WIGHT KING

• WARSCROLL •

WIGHT KING
ON SKELETAL STEED

Some Wight Kings take to battle atop ancient skeletal steeds clad in rusted barding. These Deathrattle monarchs typically ride at the very forefront of the undead advance, stampeding the enemy into dust and driving their lances into the hearts of the living.

MELEE WEAPONS	Range	Attacks	To Hit	To Wound	Rend	Damage
Tomb Lance	2"	3	3+	3+	-1	D3
Hooves and Teeth	1"	2	4+	4+	-	1

DESCRIPTION

A Wight King on Skeletal Steed is a single model armed with a Tomb Lance.

MOUNT: This model's Skeletal Steed attacks with its Hooves and Teeth.

ABILITIES

Deathly Charge: *Mounted upon its swift skeletal steed, the Wight King is capable of attaining a deadly momentum before its lance strikes home.*

After this model makes a charge move, you can pick 1 enemy unit within 1" of this model and roll a dice. On a 2+, that enemy unit suffers D3 mortal wounds.

COMMAND ABILITIES

Lord of Bones: *At the rasped command of their king, the Deathrattle hordes lay about the enemy with a tireless focus.*

You can use this command ability in your hero phase. If you do so, pick 1 friendly DEATHRATTLE unit wholly within 12" of this model. Until the end of that phase, you can re-roll hit rolls of 1 for attacks made with melee weapons by that unit.

KEYWORDS DEATH, SOULBLIGHT GRAVELORDS, DEATHRATTLE, HERO, WIGHT KING, WIGHT KING ON SKELETAL STEED

• WARSCROLL •

BLACK KNIGHTS

Black Knights are skeletal cavaliers who ride at the vanguard of the Deathrattle hosts. Clad in verdigrised armour and wielding wicked lances, they charge towards the foe, unearthly horns resounding as their lethal momentum slams home.

MELEE WEAPONS	Range	Attacks	To Hit	To Wound	Rend	Damage
Barrow Lance	2"	2	4+	3+	-	1
Hooves and Teeth	1"	2	4+	4+	-	1

DESCRIPTION

A unit of Black Knights has any number of models, each armed with a Barrow Lance.

MOUNT: This unit's Skeletal Steeds attack with their Hooves and Teeth.

CHAMPION: 1 model in this unit can be a Hellknight. Add 1 to the Attacks characteristic of that model's Barrow Lance.

STANDARD BEARER: 1 in every 5 models in this unit can be a Standard Bearer. You can re-roll rolls of 1 for the Deathless Minions battle trait for this unit while it has any Standard Bearers.

MUSICIAN: 1 in every 5 models in this unit can be a Hornblower. While this unit has any Hornblowers, charge rolls for this unit of less than 6 are treated as being 6.

ABILITIES

Deathly Charge: *Mounted upon swift skeletal steeds, the Black Knights are capable of attaining a deadly momentum before their lances strike home.*

After this unit makes a charge move, you can pick 1 enemy unit within 1" of this unit and roll a dice. On a 2+, that enemy unit suffers D3 mortal wounds.

KEYWORDS DEATH, SOULBLIGHT GRAVELORDS, DEATHRATTLE, SUMMONABLE, BLACK KNIGHTS

• WARSCROLL •

GRAVE GUARD

The elite housecarls of the Deathrattle Kingdoms, Grave Guard march into battle at the side of their lords. Their cursed blades glow with an unearthly light, wreathed in powerful deathly enchantments that allow them to kill with the merest touch.

MELEE WEAPONS	Range	Attacks	To Hit	To Wound	Rend	Damage
Wight Blade	1"	2	3+	3+	-1	1
Great Wight Blade	1"	2	3+	4+	-1	2

DESCRIPTION

A unit of Grave Guard has any number of models. The unit is armed with 1 of the following weapon options: Wight Blade and Crypt Shield; or Great Wight Blade.

CHAMPION: 1 model in this unit can be a Seneschal. Add 1 to the Attacks characteristic of that model's Wight Blade or Great Wight Blade.

STANDARD BEARER: 1 in every 10 models in this unit can be a Standard Bearer. You can re-roll rolls of 1 for the Deathless Minions battle trait for this unit while it has any Standard Bearers.

MUSICIAN: 1 in every 10 models in this unit can be a Hornblower. While this unit has any Hornblowers, charge rolls for this unit of less than 6 are treated as being 6.

ABILITIES

Cursed Weapons: *The blades wielded by the Grave Guard carry dire curses that can sever the souls from the bodies of those they touch.*

If the unmodified wound roll for an attack made with a melee weapon by this unit is 6, the target suffers 1 mortal wound in addition to any normal damage.

Crypt Shields: *Though the shields of the Grave Guard appear worn and tattered, the ancient magics bound into them are capable of resisting the more fearsome blows.*

Add 1 to save rolls for attacks that target a unit armed with Wight Blades and Crypt Shields.

KEYWORDS DEATH, SOULBLIGHT GRAVELORDS, DEATHRATTLE, SUMMONABLE, GRAVE GUARD

WARSCROLL

DEATHRATTLE SKELETONS

Skulls locked in an eternal grimace, Deathrattle Skeletons are the footsoldiers of the undead. To stand before these clattering companies demands courage, for they are the fate of mortals given form, and their rusted weapons have retained their killing edge.

MELEE WEAPONS	Range	Attacks	To Hit	To Wound	Rend	Damage
Ancient Blade or Spear	1"	1	3+	4+	-	1
Champion's Mace or Halberd	1"	2	3+	3+	-	1

DESCRIPTION

A unit of Deathrattle Skeletons has any number of models, each armed with an Ancient Blade or Spear.

CHAMPION: 1 model in this unit can be a Skeleton Champion. A Skeleton Champion can replace their Ancient Blade or Spear with a Champion's Mace or Halberd.

STANDARD BEARER: 1 in every 10 models in this unit can be a Standard Bearer. You can re-roll rolls of 1 for the Deathless Minions battle trait for this unit while it has any Standard Bearers.

ABILITIES

Skeleton Legion: *Though slow in their approach, these undead warriors rise to rejoin the fight time and time again in spite of their losses.*

When you pick this unit to fight, roll a dice for each model in this unit that was slain in that phase. On a 4+, you can return that model to this unit.

KEYWORDS DEATH, SOULBLIGHT GRAVELORDS, DEATHRATTLE, SUMMONABLE, DEATHRATTLE SKELETONS

WARSCROLL

THE SEPULCHRAL GUARD

The Sepulchral Guard haunt the Mirrored City of Shadespire, cursed by Nagash to fully appreciate their horror. Led by the Sepulchral Warden, the former Lord-Marshal of the city, they fall upon and slay interlopers with an unsettling swiftness.

MELEE WEAPONS	Range	Attacks	To Hit	To Wound	Rend	Damage
Ancient Spear	2"	3	4+	4+	-	1
Ancient Mace	1"	2	4+	3+	-	1
Ancient Greatblade	1"	2	4+	4+	-1	1
Ancient Scythe	1"	1	4+	3+	-	2
Ancient Blade	1"	1	4+	4+	-	1

DESCRIPTION

The Sepulchral Guard is a unit that has 7 models. The Sepulchral Warden is armed with an Ancient Spear; the Prince of Dust is armed with an Ancient Mace; the Champion is armed with an Ancient Greatblade; the Harvester is armed with an Ancient Scythe; and the 3 Petitioners are each armed with an Ancient Blade.

THE SEPULCHRAL WARDEN: The Sepulchral Warden has a Wounds characteristic of 2. At the start of your hero phase, if this model is on the battlefield, you can return D3 slain models to this unit.

ABILITIES

Frightening Speed: *The Sepulchral Guard move with a shocking swiftness, their motion guided by fragmented memories of their mortal lives.*

You can re-roll charge rolls for this unit.

Serve in Death: *Pitiless footsoldiers of the armies of undeath, Deathrattle Skeletons strike with unnatural zeal.*

If the unmodified hit roll for an attack made by this unit is 6, that attack scores 2 hits on the target instead of 1. Make a wound and save roll for each hit.

KEYWORDS DEATH, SOULBLIGHT GRAVELORDS, DEATHRATTLE, DEATHRATTLE SKELETONS, THE SEPULCHRAL GUARD

• WARSCROLL •

DIRE WOLVES

It is said that to hear a Dire Wolf's howl is to be damned. These lupine undead are tireless hunters, and when they finally run their prey to ground, their powerful jaws ensure that the kill comes swiftly indeed.

MELEE WEAPONS	Range	Attacks	To Hit	To Wound	Rend	Damage
Rotting Fangs and Claws	1"	2	4+	4+	-	1

DESCRIPTION

A unit of Dire Wolves has any number of models, each armed with Rotting Fangs and Claws.

CHAMPION: 1 in every 10 models in this unit must be a Doom Wolf. Add 1 to the Attacks characteristic of that model's Rotting Fangs and Claws.

ABILITIES

Slavering Charge: *A charging Dire Wolf can swiftly overwhelm its prey in a storm of snapping jaws and raking claws.*

Add 1 to hit and wound rolls for attacks made with melee weapons by this unit if it made a charge move in the same turn.

KEYWORDS DEATH, SOULBLIGHT GRAVELORDS, DEADWALKERS, SUMMONABLE, DIRE WOLVES

• WARSCROLL •

FELL BATS

Winging their way through the darkness, Fell Bats are hideous aerial predators marked by the Soulblight curse. Even the merest taste of blood sends these beasts into a frenzy; from there, only complete destruction can halt their maddened rampages.

MELEE WEAPONS	Range	Attacks	To Hit	To Wound	Rend	Damage
Elongated Fangs	1"	3	4+	4+	-	1

DESCRIPTION

A unit of Fell Bats has any number of models, each armed with Elongated Fangs.

FLY: This unit can fly.

ABILITIES

Single-minded Ferocity: *When a colony of Fell Bats descends upon the foe, they attack in waves, crashing into their prey before retreating and falling upon them again.*

This unit can retreat and still charge later in the same turn.

KEYWORDS DEATH, SOULBLIGHT GRAVELORDS, SUMMONABLE, FELL BATS

PITCHED BATTLE PROFILES

The table below provides points, unit sizes and battlefield roles for the warscrolls and warscroll battalions in this book for use in Pitched Battles. Spending the points listed in this table allows you to take a minimum-sized unit with any of its upgrades. Understrength units cost the full amount of points. Larger units are taken in multiples of their minimum unit size; multiply their cost by the same amount as you multiplied their size. If a unit has two points values separated by a slash (e.g. '60/200'), the second value is for a maximum-sized unit. Units that are listed as 'Unique' are named characters and can only be taken once in an army. A unit that has any of the keywords listed in the Allies table can be taken as an allied unit by a Soulblight Gravelords army. Updated May 2021; the profiles printed here take precedence over any profiles with an earlier publication date or no publication date.

SOULBLIGHT GRAVELORDS WARSCROLL	UNIT SIZE		POINTS	BATTLEFIELD ROLE	NOTES
	MIN	MAX			
Deathrattle Skeletons	10	30	85	Battleline	
Dire Wolves	10	30	135	Battleline	
Mortis Engine	1	1	200	Behemoth	
Terrorgheist	1	1	305	Behemoth	Battleline if AVENGORII DYNASTY
Zombie Dragon	1	1	295	Behemoth	Battleline if AVENGORII DYNASTY
Gorslav the Gravekeeper	1	1		Leader	
Radukar the Wolf	1	1		Leader	Unique. These units must be taken as a set for 755 points. Although taken as a set, each is a separate unit.
Torgillius the Chamberlain	1	1		Leader	
Watch Captain Halgrim	1	1	755	Leader	
Kosargi Nightguard	2	2			
Vargskyr	1	1			
Vyrkos Blood-born	3	3			
Prince Duvalle	1	1		Leader	Unique. These units must be taken as a set for a total of 200 points. Although taken as a set, each is a separate unit.
The Crimson Court	3	3	200		
Belladamma Volga, First of the Vyrkos	1	1	200	Leader	Unique
Kritza, the Rat Prince	1	1	95	Leader	Unique
Lady Annika, the Thirsting Blade	1	1	110	Leader	Unique
Lauka Vai, Mother of Nightmares	1	1	285	Leader	Unique
Necromancer	1	1	125	Leader	
Radukar the Beast	1	1	315	Leader	Unique. This model cannot be part of the same army as Radukar the Wolf.
Vampire Lord	1	1	140	Leader	
Vengorian Lord	1	1	280	Leader	
Wight King	1	1	115	Leader	
Wight King on Skeletal Steed	1	1	130	Leader	
Bloodseeker Palanquin	1	1	290	Leader, Behemoth	
Coven Throne	1	1	310	Leader, Behemoth	
Mannfred von Carstein, Mortarch of Night	1	1	380	Leader, Behemoth	Unique
Nagash, Supreme Lord of the Undead	1	1	975	Leader, Behemoth	Unique
Neferata, Mortarch of Blood	1	1	365	Leader, Behemoth	Unique
Prince Vhordrai	1	1	455	Leader, Behemoth	Unique
Vampire Lord on Zombie Dragon	1	1	435	Leader, Behemoth	
Black Knights	5	15	120		Battleline if LEGION OF BLOOD
Blood Knights	5	15	195		Battleline if KASTELAI DYNASTY
Corpse Cart with Balefire Brazier	1	1	80		
Corpse Cart with Unholy Lodestone	1	1	80		
Deadwalker Zombies	20	40	115		Battleline in a Soulblight Gravelords army
Fell Bats	3	9	75		
Grave Guard	10	30	140		Battleline if general is WIGHT KING
The Sepulchral Guard	7	7	80		Unique
Vargheists	3	9	155		Battleline if LEGION OF NIGHT
Deathmarch	-	-	*120*	*Warscroll Battalion*	
Deathstench Drove	-	-	*100*	*Warscroll Battalion*	
Fellwing Flock	-	-	*80*	*Warscroll Battalion*	
Legion of Shyish	-	-	*60*	*Warscroll Battalion*	
Red Banqueters	-	-	*100*	*Warscroll Battalion*	

FACTION	ALLIES
Soulblight Gravelords	Flesh-eater Courts, Nighthaunt